Beginning Excel VBA Programming

A concise guide to developing Excel VBA Applications and Macros

---

2nd Edition
Iducate Learning Technologies

Chapter 1: Introduction to Excel VBA 1
Your First Excel VBA Program 2
Input and Output in VBA 3

Chapter 2: Variables 5
Variable Data Types 5
Operations on Variables 7
Volume Calculator Example 7

Chapter 3: If-Else, Select Case Statements 10
Multiple Conditions 11
If-Else-If 12
Select Case 13

Chapter 4: Loops 15
Nested For-Next Loops 17
Do-While Loop 18
For Each Loop 18
Looping Through Selection of Cells 19

Chapter 5: Subroutines and Functions 20
Functions 22
What's the difference then? 23

Chapter 6: Debugging Excel VBA 25
Setting Break Points 25
Step Over 26
Step Into 29

Chapter 7: Using Worksheet Functions 32
Commonly used Financial Functions 32
Common Statistical Functions 33
Common Math, Trigonometry Functions 33
Common Text Functions 35

Chapter 8: Referring and Operating on Things in Excel 37

Chapter 9: Recording Macros 39
Macro Code Generation in Real Time 41

Chapter 10: Creating User Forms 43
Adding Buttons 51
Implementing the Button's Event Handler 53
Implementing the Form 56
Calling our Form 58

Chapter 11: More User Form Controls 61

Chapter 12: Using Event Handlers 68
Using Worksheet Event Handlers 68
Using Workbook Event Handlers 72

Chapter 13: Retrieving Data from the Web 74

Chapter 14: Real World Case - Simple Financial Modeling Using Excel VBA 81
Stock Valuation using Excel 81
Creating the Stock Valuation Model using Excel VBA 84

Going Further 89

Copyright © 2011 by Iducate Learning Technologies

All rights reserved. No part of this publication may be reproduced, distributed, or transmitted in any form or by any means, including photocopying, recording, or other electronic or mechanical methods, without the prior written permission of the publisher, except in the case of brief quotations embodied in critical reviews and certain other noncommercial uses permitted by copyright law.

2nd Edition

Chapter 1: Introduction to Excel VBA

Excel as you might already be familiar with is a spreadsheet program from Microsoft. It is not the aim of this book to teach you about Excel features, e.g. Cells, Ranges, but rather, to explore the often neglected yet extremely powerful programming feature of Excel which is Visual Basic programming. The Visual Basic programming component is more often referred to as Excel VBA.

Excel VBA allows one to create Excel spreadsheets much more powerful than if one just sticks to cell, ranges, formulas and charts. It is particular used in the financial industry where trading spreadsheets and financial models are built using Excel VBA.

Some functions that Excel VBA can provide are, complex calculations, taking in user input, dynamic output, automation, connection to databases, designing professional looking user forms and much more!

Figure 1 shows the spreadsheet features of Excel.

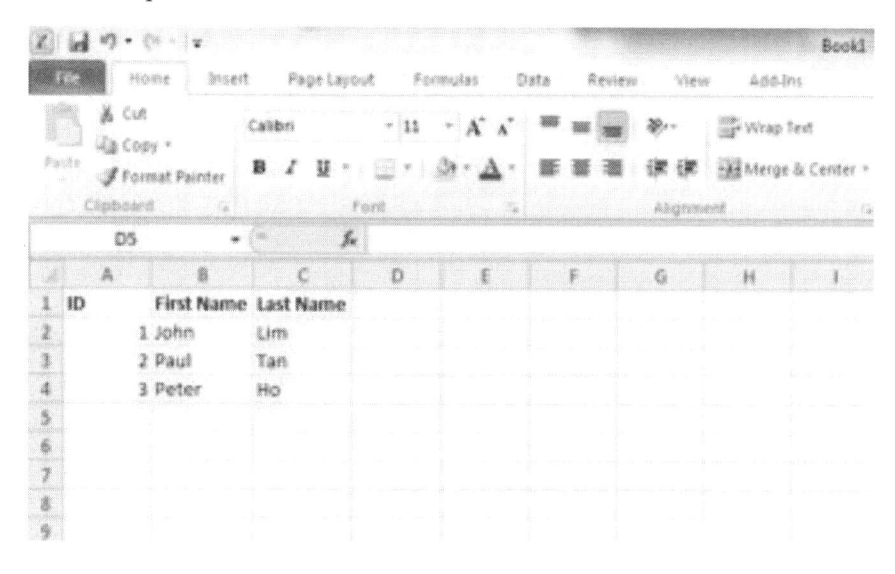

Figure 1 – Spreadsheet Features of Excel

To explore the powerful programming side of Excel VBA, press Alt – F11. This will open up the Visual Basic Editor (VBE) which provides the programming features in Excel (Figure 2).

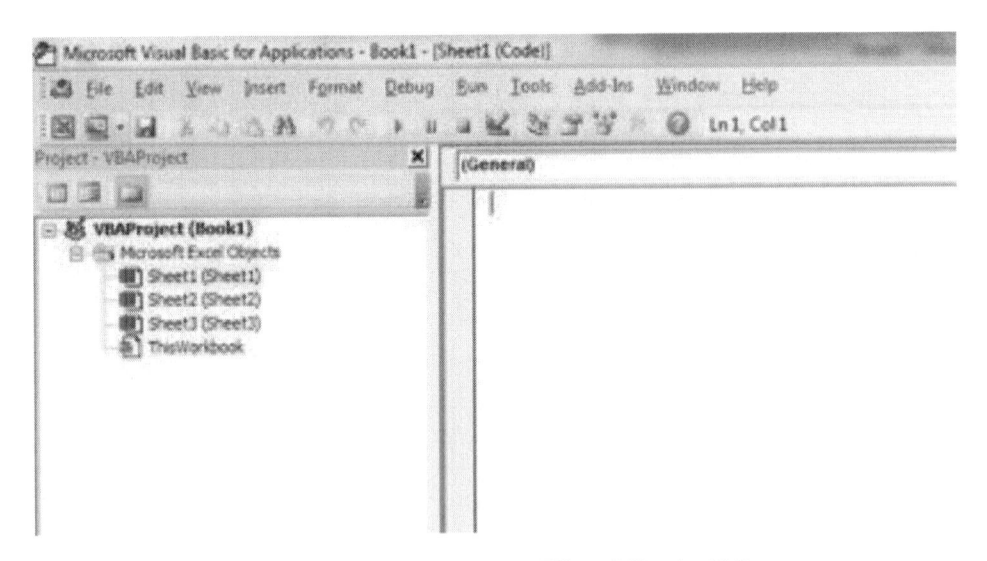

Figure 2 - Visual Basic Editor

In the left side of the VBE, you have the Project Explorer which lists down the worksheets that you have in your Excel sheet.

On the right, you have the Code Editor which shows you the VBA code for the selected sheet in the Project Explorer.

Now let's get on with building our first Excel VBA program!

Excel VBA can be used powerfully to solve everyday problems. We will go through a simple example.

Your First Excel VBA Program
Write a program to calculate and print the area of a circle.

Thus, if we input a radius of 5 cm, the output will be 78.5 cm sq.

Enter the following code below into the code editor.

```
Sub calculateArea()
        'read radius
        Radius = InputBox("Enter radius:")

        Pi = 3.142

        'calculate Area
        area = Pi * Radius * Radius

        'Output area on screen
        MsgBox "Area is " & area
End Sub
```

Click on the '**Run**' button (Figure 4).

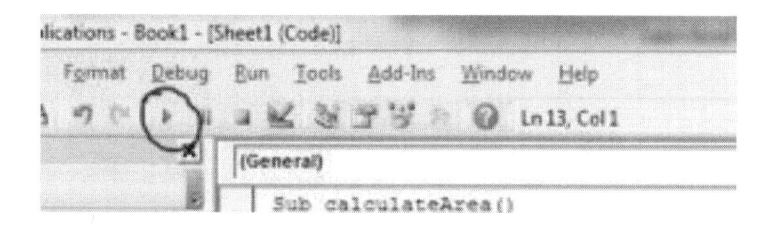

Figure 4 - Run button

You should see the **Input Box** appearing prompting you to enter a radius (Figure 5).

Figure 5 - Input box for radius

Enter a radius value and click on '**Ok**'. A **MessageBox** will appear with the calculated area.

Figure 6 - MessageBox for output of area

Congratulations! You have just programmed your first Excel VBA program.

Input and Output in VBA

Notice that in your program, you have used

Radius = InputBox("Enter radius:")

to read in user input for radius? A common way for input is using **InputBox**. It will open an InputBox with the message supplied to it, in our case, it is "Enter radius". And whatever we enter into the inputBox is assigned to the Radius variable. (More on variables in the next chapter.)

Notice also that we use **MsgBox** for output.

MsgBox "Area is " & area

MsgBox opens a popup box which shows "Area is " followed by the calculated area. The '&' joins the String "Area is " together with the calculated area. More on '&' in the following chapters.

In Summary

You have explored with the vba editor in Excel and have coded your first macro! What we have introduced is just the tip of the iceberg in Excel VBA programming. We have only started this exciting journey and will bring you much more exciting chapters as you read on. Now let's go on to the next chapter to learn about variables.

Chapter 2: Variables

Variables are a fundamental concept in programming. You might not recall using variables before, but you have in fact used them in Elementary Math Algebra. Remember when the teacher first taught you

x = 2?

x is a variable in this case. And *x* stores the value of 2. **Variables are used to store data.** In the earlier example where we calculated the area of a circle, the variable '*Pi*' was used to store the value of 3.142.

Pi = 3.142

The variable '*radius*' was used to store the user input radius value.

Radius = InputBox("Enter radius:")

Variable Data Types

Variables can have different data types. Data types means 'type of data'. In the previous example, '*Radius*' and '*Pi*' both have the same data type of **Double**. Double refers to a number with decimals. Other data type include:

Integer or **Long** – which represents whole numbers
Single or **Double** – which represents numbers with decimals
String – names or words e.g. *a, b, x, y, efg*
Boolean – true or false values

It is important that you know the data type of a variable. For example, the data type for '*Radius*' cannot be a String.

In the *calculateArea()* program, we did not declare data types for our variables. Excel VBA does not make it mandatory for us to declare variable data types. However, we should still do so as it might introduce errors in our code which are hard to detect.

Sub calculateArea()
    'read radius
    Radius = InputBox("Enter radius:")

    Pi = 3.142

    'calculate Area
    *area = Pi * Radius * Radius*

    'Output area on screen

```
        MsgBox "Area is " & area
End Sub
```

Hence, our code for *calculateArea()* with proper declaration of variable types instead should be like in below.

```
Sub calculateArea()
        Dim Radius As Double
        Dim Pi As Double
        Dim area As Double

        'read radius
        Radius = InputBox("Enter radius:")

        Pi = 3.142

        'calculate Area
        area = Pi * Radius * Radius

        'Output area on screen
        MsgBox "Area is " & area
End Sub
```

Code 7 - Program with proper declaration of variable data types

We use the keyword '*Dim*' to declare a variable followed by the variable's name, and next specify the data type with '*As Double*'.

Hence, the format should be,

Dim <variable name> As <data type>

Examples:

Dim Radius As Double
Dim name As String
Dim age As Integer

But how do we know which data type to use in variables? If you need to perform calculations on it, e.g. radius, area, the data type is probably **Integer** or **Double**.

If you want to store names, sentences, words, it will be **String**.

Operations on Variables

You can perform operations on variables for e.g. adding/subtracting/multiplying/dividing two variables using **operators**. Again we probably have learned that in elementary math. Operators are things like '+', '-', '*', '/', '='.

For e.g.:

a + b computes the sum of *a* and *b*
c = 8 changes the value of *c* to 8
c = a + b computes the sum of *a* and *b* and assigns the result to *c*.

Other than mathematical operations, we can perform concatenation operations on **Strings**. In other words, we can join two words together with the operator '&'.

In the earlier *calculateArea()* example, we join the output message of *"Area is "* with *area* using '&'

"Area is " & area

Another example,

s = "Cry" & "Baby" will return us the value of *"CryBaby"*

Volume Calculator Example

Let's go through an example of solving a problem using variables and operators.

Problem: Calculate the volume of a cone given its base radius and height.

To calculate volume of a cone, recall that the formula is 1/3 * pi * radius * radius * height.

We would first read input from user for radius and height. However, this time round, we will not be using the **InputBox** method. We will let user enter the values in the worksheet cells and thereafter read the values directly from the cells (Figure 8). We will also write the calculated volume to the worksheet straight instead of using the MessageBox.

	A	B
1	Pi	3.14
2	r	0.5
3	h	1.5
4	v	0.3925
5		

Figure 8 - Read in values from Cells

We first declare the variables and their data type (Code 9). Data type of Double would be most appropriate here since we are performing calculations that have decimals.

```
Sub calculateVol()
    Dim pi As Double
    Dim r As Double
    Dim h As Double
    Dim v As Double
End Sub
```

Code 9 - Declaration of variables and their data type

Next, we read in values from the worksheet cells using *Cells(<row>,<column>).Value*. How Cells().Value work is that we provide the row and column of the cell and use the *Value* property to return us the value in that cell.

For example, the value of 3.14 for pi is in cell B1 which is in row 1, column 2. Hence the code to extract the value of pi is,

pi = Cells(1, 2).Value

```
Sub calculateVol()
    Dim pi As Double
    Dim r As Double
    Dim h As Double
    Dim v As Double

    'read in values from cells
    pi = Cells(1,2).Value
    r = Cells(2,2).Value
    h = Cells(3,2).Value
End Sub
```

Code 10 - reading values from cells & assigning them to variables

We next calculate the volume of the cone with operators '*', '^', '/'.

*v = (pi * r ^ 2 * h) / 3*

Lastly, we output the calculated volume *v* by assigning its value to the output cell in row 4, column 2.

Cells(4, 2).Value = v

```
Sub calculateVol()
    Dim pi As Double
    Dim r As Double
    Dim h As Double
    Dim v As Double

    'read in values from cells
```

```
pi = Cells(1,2).Value
r = Cells(2,2).Value
h = Cells(3,2).Value

'calculate volume
v = (pi * r ^ 2 * h)/3

'output volume to cell
Cells(4,2).Value = v
End Sub
```

Code 11 - calculate volume and output result to cell

Throughout the code, you might have noticed phrase beginning with the single apostrophe like
'read in values from cells

These are **comments**. They do not affect the code in any way but helps the programmer to describe the code which will help another person to understand the code easier. You should aim to provide meaningful comments in your code.

In Summary

You have learned the usage of variables, how you can use them to receive user input, calculate complex formulas and output the result back to the worksheet.

Going further, think of how you can extend this to more complicated scenarios and formulas like calculating the price of a stock or the monthly interest you have to pay for taking a loan.

Chapter 3: If-Else, Select Case Statements

We often have to make decisions. That applies to our programs as well. For example, if marks are less than 50, it means a fail. Else, it's a pass. Excel VBA allows us to make decisions with the *If-Else* Statement.

The below shows an example of a VBA program using *If-Else* statement.

```
Sub passFailCheck()
   Dim marks As Double
   marks = InputBox("Enter marks")

   If marks < 50 Then
      MsgBox "Failed!"
   Else
      MsgBox "Passed!"
   End If
End Sub
```

Code 12 - If Else statement

Try running the program. Notice that when you enter a number lesser than 50, you get the message box with the message "Failed!" and when you enter a number greater than or equal to 50, you get the message "Passed!".

That is the If-Else statement at work. Based on the condition *marks < 50*, if the condition is true, it will output "Failed." Else, it will output "Passed!"

In general, the statement for an If-Else code is

```
If <condition> Then
        <code to execute when condition is true>
Else
        <code to execute when condition is false>
End If
```

Our condition in the above example was *marks < 50*.
A condition can only evaluate to TRUE or FALSE.

2 + 3 is not a condition. It evaluates to 5.

marks = 75 is a condition. It represents the condition that marks must equal 75.

More examples of conditions:

marks <> 60. The condition is that marks must not be equal to 60.
marks < 55. The condition is that marks must be less than 55.
marks <= 55. The condition is that marks must be less than **or equal** to 55.
marks > 55. The condition is that marks must be more than 55.
marks >= 55. The condition is that marks must be more than **or equal** to 55.

Below shows another example this time using If-Else statements to check for fever by checking the condition if temperature is above 37 (degrees Celsius).

Sub feverCheck()
  Dim temperature As Double
  temperature = InputBox("Enter temperature")

  If temperature > 37 Then
    MsgBox "You have a fever!"
  Else
    MsgBox "You do not have a fever!"
  End If
End Sub

Code 13 - Fever check using If-Else

Multiple Conditions

The previous examples only show a single condition. Suppose we have to check if marks are more than equal to 70 and less than 80 for a 'B+' grade?

We can check for multiple conditions using the **And** and **Or** operators. The below code shows an example where we use the **And** operator to check for a B+ grade which is between 70 and 80 marks.

Sub gradeCheck()
  Dim marks As Double
  marks = InputBox("Enter marks")

  If marks >= 70 And marks < 80 Then
    MsgBox "Grade B+!"
  Else
    MsgBox "Other grades."

End If
End Sub

Code 14 - Using the And operator to check for multiple conditions

Code 15 shows an example where we use the **Or** operator to check for passing of a subject. If either a student scores less than 50 or his attendance is less than 50 percent, he will fail.

Sub gradeCheck()
   Dim marks As Double
   Dim attendancePct As Integer

   marks = InputBox("Enter marks")
   attendancePct = InputBox("Enter attendance percentage:")

   If marks < 50 Or attendancePct < 50 Then
      MsgBox "Failed course"
   Else
      MsgBox "Passed."
   End If
End Sub

Code 15 - Using the Or operator to check multiple conditions

If-Else-If

Multiple conditions can also be implemented using the *If-Else-If* statement. The If-Else-If statement is simply an extension of the *If-Else* statement. Its format is,

If <condition #1> Then
         <code to execute when condition #1 is true>
ElseIf <condition #2> Then
         <code to execute when condition #2 is true>
ElseIf <condition #3 ...(if necessary)> Then
         <code to execute when condition #3 is true>
...
Else
         <code to execute when all conditions are not met>
End If

Code 16 shows an example of using the *If-Else-If* statement to check for individual categories of grades based on marks. The code will first check the first condition, else if it is not less than 50, proceed to check for the next condition if it is less than 59 and so on, until if all conditions are not met, it will go to the last *Else* block.

Once any condition is met, e.g. <= 59, the code will break out from the If-Else-If block. It will not go on to evaluate the rest of the conditions.

```
Sub gradeCheck()
    Dim marks As Double
    marks = InputBox("Enter marks")

    If marks < 50 Then
        MsgBox "F"
    ElseIf marks <= 59 Then
        MsgBox "D"
    ElseIf marks <= 69 Then
        MsgBox "C"
    ElseIf marks <= 79 Then
        MsgBox "B"
    Else
        MsgBox "A"
    End If
End Sub
```

Code 16 - Grade check using If-Else-If statement

Select Case

Other than using *If-Else-If*, we can also use the *Select Case* statement in a similar fashion. Code 17 shows the use of the Select Case statement to solve the same problem.

```
Sub gradeCheck()
    Dim marks As Double
    marks = InputBox("Enter marks")

    Select Case marks
        Case Is < 50
            MsgBox "F"
        Case Is <= 59
            MsgBox "D"
        Case Is <= 69
            MsgBox "C"
        Case Is <= 79
            MsgBox "B"
        Case Else
            MsgBox "A"
```

```
    End Select
End Sub
```

Code 17 - Using Select Case

Once any condition is met, e.g. <= 59, the code will break out from the Select Case block. It will not go on to evaluate the rest of the conditions.

In situations where we want to execute specific code based on the value of a **SINGLE** variable, *Select Case* is a better choice than *If-Else-If*.

An alternative usage of Select Case to solve the same problem is shown in Code 18. Instead of having <= 59, we make use of the *To* keyword e.g. *Case 50 To 59*

```
Sub gradeCheck()
    Dim marks As Double

    marks = InputBox("Enter marks")

    Select Case marks
        Case 0 To 50
            MsgBox "F"
        Case 50 To 59
            MsgBox "D"
        Case 60 To 69
            MsgBox "C"
        Case 70 To 79
            MsgBox "B"
        Case Else
            MsgBox "A"
    End Select
End Sub
```

Code 18 - Alternative Usage of Select Case

In Summary

You have learned how to create macros that can make decisions based on variable values using the If-Else and Select Case statement.

Thinking of how this can be useful in calculating taxes payable for different income tax brackets or calculating the total price of concert tickets where there are different charges for children, adults and seniors.

Chapter 4: Loops

When we want to execute a statement **multiple** times, for e.g., populate multiple rows/columns, read multiple rows/columns with data, we can use loops.

Loops are one of the most powerful structures in programming. In Excel VBA, we can implement loops using the **For-Next** and **While Wend** loop. Code 19 shows an example of a *For Next* loop.

```
Sub sampleForNextLoop()
    For i=1 To 100
        Cells(i,2).Value = "Hello"
    Next i
End Sub
```

Code 19 - Example For-Next Loop

The above loop will print "Hello" a hundred times in column B (Figure 20).

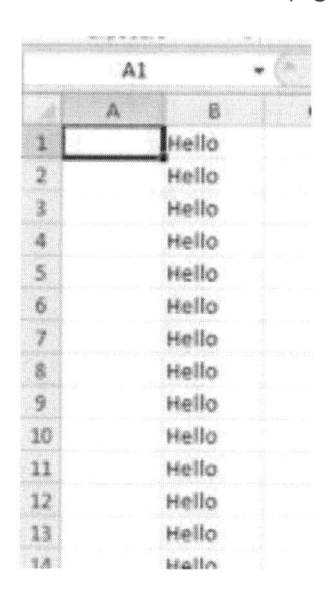

Figure 20 - Printing "Hello" 100 times in column B

The format for a *For-Next* loop is

For <starting condition> To <ending condition>
    Loop body
Next <increment counter>

In our case, our starting condition is *i = 1*. That is, we have a variable *i* which starts from the value of 1. Ending condition is *100*. The loop will continue till *i* is 100.
The loop body is *Cells(i,2).Value = "Hello"*. As explained before, *Cells(i,2)* refers to the cell in the *i*th row,

15

2nd column. Hence, the value in that cell will be the String "Hello".
Our increment counter will be *Next i*. This means that i will be incremented by 1 each time in each iteration of the loop. Hence, what will happen is that we will have *Cells(1,2).Value = "Hello"*, *Cells(2,2).Value = "Hello"*… … *Cells(100,2).Value = "Hello"* being executed.

Another example is shown in Code 21,
Sub sampleForNextLoop2()
  For j = 1 To 100
    ActiveCell.Offset(j, 0) = Rnd
  Next j
End Sub

Code 21 - Sample For Next loop populating random values

In code 21, the loop variable name is changed to *j* instead of *I* (you can name it anything you want!). The rest of the conditions remain similar. The loop body is however changed to
ActiveCell.Offset(j,0) = Rnd.
Rnd is a function that returns you a random number.
ActiveCell.Offset(<row>,<col>) refers to the number of rows and columns away from the current active cell. Hence, the above loop will print random numbers in the next 100 rows below the current cell.

Sub sampleForNextLoop2()
  For j = 1 To 100 Step 2
    ActiveCell.Offset(j, 0) = Rnd
  Next j
End Sub

Code 22 – Loop with increment of 2

We can do a slight modification and add '*Step 2*' after the ending condition.

*For j = 1 To 100 **Step 2***

For this loop, we get the following result show in Figure 23.

16

0.742342

0.840887

0.278389

0.70297

0.404865

0.811571

0.741781

Figure 23 - Results of loop - Step 2

What we are doing is that our loop's iteration counter is 1,3,5,7... instead of 1,2,3,4,5...in the earlier example. We increment in multiples of 2 rather than incrementing by 1.

Nested For-Next Loops

We can have nested For-Next loops as well. This is simply a For-Next loop in a For-Next loop like in code 24.

```
Sub nestedForNextLoop()
    For Col = 1 To 5
        For Row = 1 To 10
            Cells(Row, Col) = Rnd
        Next Row
    Next Col
End Sub
```

Code 24 - Nested For Next Loop

What this loop does is that it fills in random values for cells columns 1 to 5 for 10 rows (Figure 25).

This is particular useful when you need to read/populate a range of cells both spanning multiple rows and columns.

	A	B	C	D	E
1	0.195535	0.991402	0.010293	0.028247	0.207594
2	0.326157	0.471391	0.151657	0.827899	0.364688
3	0.413233	0.00402	0.377408	0.783374	0.57352
4	0.152677	0.425849	0.188132	0.791155	0.344181
5	0.619832	0.288717	0.979531	0.332691	0.52823
6	0.09941	0.752542	0.872118	0.450942	0.425485
7	0.205047	0.891279	0.581503	0.555113	0.573013
8	0.692518	0.821931	0.729411	0.80333	0.050045
9	0.504459	0.176887	0.145	0.563989	0.5476
10	0.183076	0.108786	0.25779	0.203582	0.206485

Figure 25 - Range of Cells populated by Nested For loop

Do-While Loop

We can also implement loops using the *Do-While* loop structure. The *Do-While* loop is slightly different from the *For-Next* loop in that the *Do-While* loop continues **till a specified condition is met**.

Sub doWhileLoop()
  Do While ActiveCell.Value <> Empty
    ActiveCell.Value = "!!!"
    ActiveCell.Offset(1, 0).Select
  Loop
End Sub

Code 26 - Do While loop example

Code 26 shows a loop which will loop through a column and if the cell's value is not empty, it will populate that cell with the value "!!!". The loop will go on to the next row's cell with the *ActiveCell.Offset(1, 0).SelectOffset(1,0)* will set it to the next row and select will make that next row's cell the active(current) cell.

The loop will end when it encounters an empty cell.

For Each Loop

We can use loops to access workbooks, worksheets, ranges and cells too using the **For-Each** loop! In Code 27, we loop through each worksheet in the current workbook and delete the first row in each worksheet.

Sub deleteRowInEveryWorksheet()
  Dim wkSht As Worksheet

  For Each wkSht In ActiveWorkbook.Worksheets
    wkSht.Rows(1).Delete

Next wkSht
End Sub

Code 27 - Looping through worksheets

Notice that the *For-Each* loop does not have a variable to store the counter (e.g. *For i = 1 To 10*). This is because the *For-Each* loop automatically loops through all the elements in it.

Looping Through Selection of Cells

To loop through a selection of cells, you loop through the individual cells. Code 28 shows an example of looping through a selection and setting the font of the cell to bold if the value of the cell is more than zero.

Sub loopingRange()
   Dim cell As Range

   For Each cell In Selection
     If cell.Value > 0 Then
       cell.Font.Bold = True
     End If
   Next cell
End Sub

Code 28 - Looping through a Selection of Cells

In Summary

You have learned how to use loops to iterate through a range of cells to read, write or edit their values. Think of how this could be useful in iterating through a set of stock returns and highlighting negative returns in red and positive returns in green.

Chapter 5: Subroutines and Functions

So far, in the VBA programs you have written, noticed that they are always enclosed in

Sub <name>
   ...
End Sub

The word *Sub* stands for sub routine. A sub routine is a group of code that performs a specific function. So far, our programs have consisted of only one sub routine because our programs have been small. But Excel VBA allows for multiple sub routines. This is necessary when our program gets bigger and there needs to have various functions which will make our code very messy if we were to put everything in one sub routine.

For example, we can make use of a subroutine that calculates area of a circle when asking user input for radius.

```
Sub calculateArea()
    Dim radius As Double
    Dim area As Double

    'read radius
    radius = InputBox("Enter radius:")

    'calculate area
    Call calculateCircleArea(area, radius)

    'Output area on screen
    MsgBox "Area is " & area
End Sub


Sub calculateCircleArea(area, radius)
    pi = 3.142

    'calculate area
    area = pi * radius * radius
End Sub
```

Code 51 - Calling a Sub Routine

In Code 51, we have two sub routines, *calculateArea*, and *calculateCircleArea*. The sub routine *calculateArea* is responsible mainly for taking user input radius.

Dim radius As Double
Dim area As Double
'read radius
radius = InputBox("Enter radius:")

It will then it will call sub routine *calculateCircleArea*.

'calculate area
Call calculateCircleArea(area, radius)

Notice that the **Call** keyword is used to call another subroutine. Also, notice that we have **arguments** *area* and *radius* in the brackets of the call. The *area* variable is passed to the subroutine to store the result of the calculated area. The radius variable is used to pass the user input value to the subroutine for calcation.

calculateCircleArea is solely responsible for calculating the area of the circle.

Sub calculateCircleArea(area, radius)
  pi = 3.142
  'calculate area
  *area = pi * radius * radius*
End Sub

Once the *calculateCircleArea* has finished calculating, it will return the result back to *calculateArea* with the variable *area* which already stores the result.
  *area = pi * radius * radius*
End Sub

calculateArea will finally output the area in a message box.
  'Output area on screen
  MsgBox "Area is " & area
End Sub

In summary, sub routines are used to perform specific functions like *calculateCircleArea*. We might have another sub routine called *calculateConeVol* or *calculateSphereVol*.

Subroutines can also accept arguments like *calculateCircleArea(area, radius)* for values to be passed to the subroutine from the calling sub routine e.g. *radius*. Results can also be returned using the arguments e.g. *area*.

Functions

Other than sub routines, we can also use **functions** in a similar manner to calling sub routines. See Code 52 for the same problem implemented using functions.

```
Sub calculateArea()
    Dim radius As Double
    Dim area As Double

    'read radius
    radius = InputBox("Enter radius:")

    'calculate area
    area = calculateCircleArea(radius)

    'Output area on screen
    MsgBox "Area is " & area
End Sub


Function calculateCircleArea(radius)
    pi = 3.142

    'calculate area
    calculateCircleArea = pi * radius * radius
End Function
```

Code 52 - Using Functions

The differences are as follows.

First, when declaring a function, instead of using the header *Sub*, we use the keyword **Function**.

```
Function calculateCircleArea(radius)
    pi = 3.142
    'calculate area
    calculateCircleArea = pi * radius * radius
End Function
```

Second, to call the function, instead of
Call calculateCircleArea(area, radius), we use
area = calculateCircleArea(radius)
There is no need to use the **Call** keyword in calling a function.

Third, notice that we do not have to pass in the area variable to store the output.
*Call calculateCircleArea(**area**, radius)* 'Sub routine

area = calculateCircleArea(radius) 'Function

This is because a function returns its output through its function name.

Function calculateCircleArea(radius)
  pi = 3.142
  'calculate area
  calculateCircleArea = pi * radius * radius
End Function

The calculated area value is assigned to the function name *calculateCircleArea*.

What's the difference then?

You might ask, being so similar, what's the difference then? Functions other than being used in VBA, it can also be called from the worksheet.

If you implement the function under **Modules** in the **Project Explorer** (Figure 53), you can call the function from the worksheet (Figure 54) just like you call other built-in functions like *Sum()*. We will introduce how to access built in functions from VBA code in chapter 6.

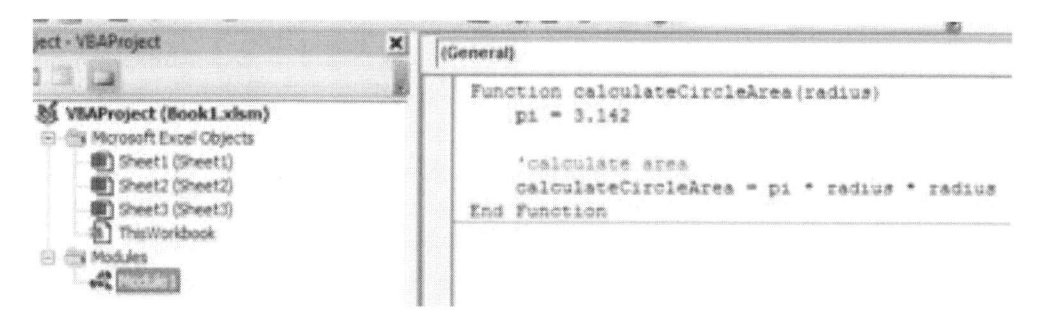

Figure 53 - Implementing Functions in 'Modules'

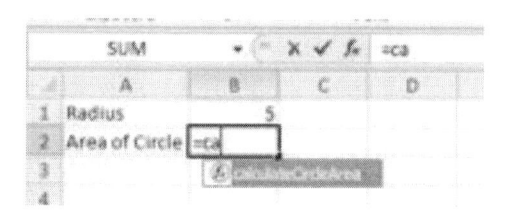

Figure 54 - Calling Functions from the Worksheet

Hence, imagine you can create your own customized functions and call it from your worksheet just like how you call *sum, average, power* etc.!

In Summary

You have learned how to implement Sub Routines and Functions. With this, you can have better structure in organizing your code into specific sub routines for a particular purpose. This also allows for better maintenance as you update and improve the spreadsheet through time. Not to forget, you have also learned how to implement your own custom Functions usable right in your worksheet!

Chapter 6: Debugging Excel VBA

You are most certain to encounter errors in your vba code. Perhaps you have already done so and are pulling out your hair over a seemingly unsolvable bug. So what to do?

Excel VBA provides a debugging function that lets you run code line by line so that you can analyze the values of variables as the code runs. Such is useful especially when you are debugging complex codes which involves if-else and loops. Let's go through an example to illustrate usage of the debugger in Excel VBA.

Below is a code which we have used in the 'Loops' chapter.

Sub sampleDebugging()

   For i = 1 To 5

      Cells(i, 2).Value = "Hello"

   Next i

End Sub

Normally, we will run this code and the loop will run by itself. Now using the debugging function, we can run this loop line by lone and examine the value of variables while the loop is going on!

Setting Break Points

First, in the vba editor, insert a break point by clicking on the left margin as shown below in fig 27. A dot will appear. Note that i am using the Mac version in this chapter but it should the same as in the windows version i.e. the dot is red color instead of pink.

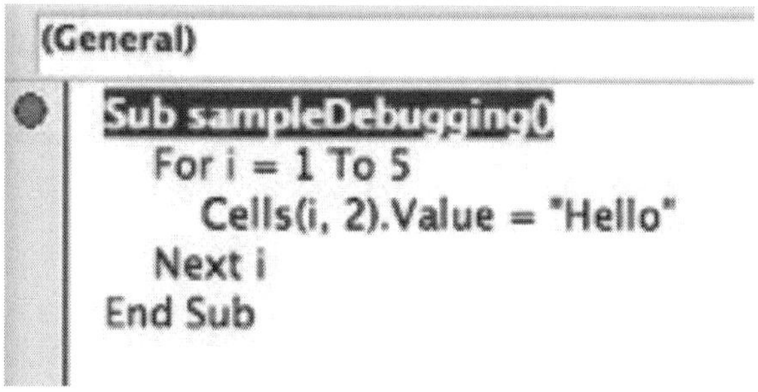

fig. 27

Next, run the macro. Notice that the line with the breakpoint is highlighted in yellow (fig. 28). What has happened is that when you place a break point in your code, you are saying that you want the execution of the program to stop at that line. Thus when the macro runs, the execution stops at that line and highlights it in yellow indicating that it is the next line to be run. Note that the highlighted line has not been run but rather, it will be the next line to run.

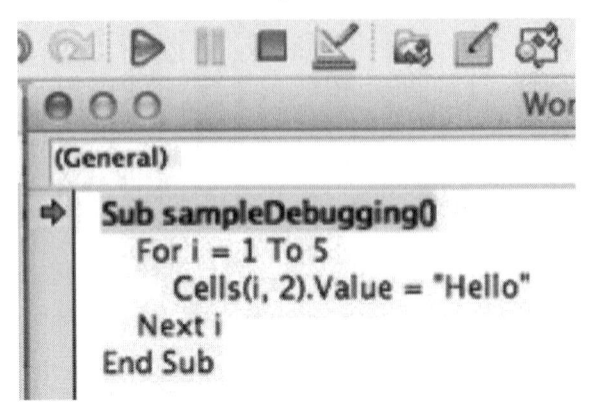

fig. 28

Step Over

Now that we have halted the execution of the macro, how do we go on to the next line? Under 'Debug', click on 'Step Over' (fig. 28b).

fig. 28b

When you do so, notice that the highlighted line in yellow moves to the next line (fig. 28c). What has happened is that the execution moves on to the next line.

26

```
Sub sampleDebugging()
    For i = 1 To 5
        Cells(i, 2).Value = "Hello"
    Next i
End Sub
```

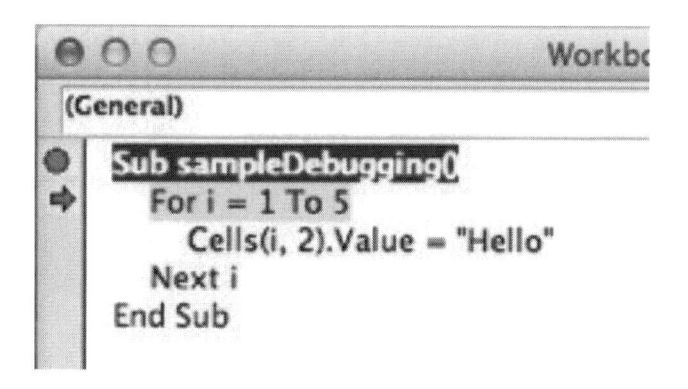

fig. 28c

As you click on 'Step Over' again (alternatively, you can use the shortcut, its must faster!), the execution goes on to the next line (fig. 28d).

```
Sub sampleDebugging()
    For i = 1 To 5
        Cells(i, 2).Value = "Hello"
    Next i
End Sub
```

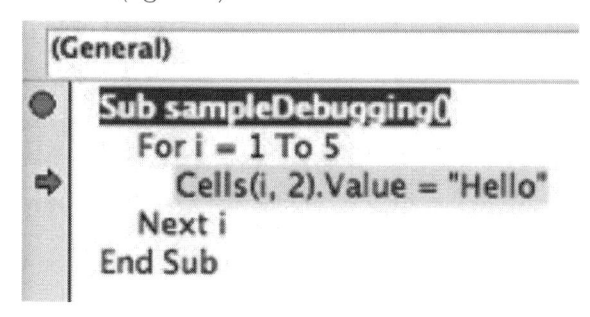

fig. 28d

Click on 'Step Over' again and look at your spreadsheet. After the line has been execution, 'Hello' gets printed on cell B1 (fig. 29).

	A	B
1		Hello
2		
3		
4		

fig. 29

So you see, the 'Step Over' function steps over to the next line of code execution. Trying stepping over by yourself and you can see as the code runs line by line that it heads back to the beginning of the loop body and carries on to the end and back to the beginning till 'i' becomes 5.

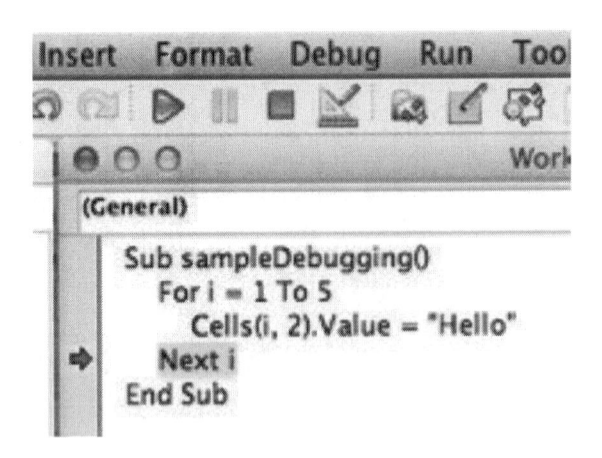

fig. 29b

Also, while you are doing this, notice that 'Hello' gets printed in column B one cell at a time as you are stepping over the program (fig. 29c, 29d).

fig. 29c

fig. 29d

Another powerful feature in the debugger is that when you 'mouse over' any variable, you can see its value. Run the macro again and put a break point on 'Next i' (fig. 30). As that line gets highlighted, mouse over the variable 'i' and notice that the editor tells you with a tooltip the value of 'i'.

28

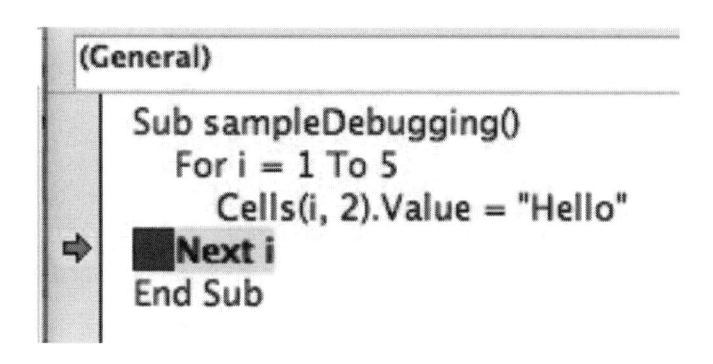

```
(General)
    Sub sampleDebugging()
        For i = 1 To 5
            Cells(i, 2).Value = "Hello"
➡       Next i
    End Sub
```

fig. 30

Thus, you can see what the debugger function is a very powerful function which lets you dissect complex code by running it line by line and letting you examine variable values so that you can know where something has gone wrong. You no longer have to print message boxes to detect bugs!

Step Into

We have illustrated the 'Step Over' function which is a straight forward function to go to the next line. But what about if your code is calling another sub routine or function? If you 'step over', you will completely skip that internal sub routine call. How do you 'step into' the inner subroutine?

Consider the following code.

Sub firstSub()

  MsgBox "In first sub"

  secondSub

End Sub

Sub secondSub()

  MsgBox "In second sub"

End Sub

In firstSub(), we print a MsgBox followed by a call to secondSub(). If you 'step over' secondSub, the debugger will not bring you to the code in secondSub(). The solution in such cases where you want to go into the called sub routine is to use 'step into' (fig. 31). When secondSub() call is highlighted, click on 'Step Into'. Notice that instead of stepping over, the debugger will bring you to the 'secondSub' (fig. 31b).

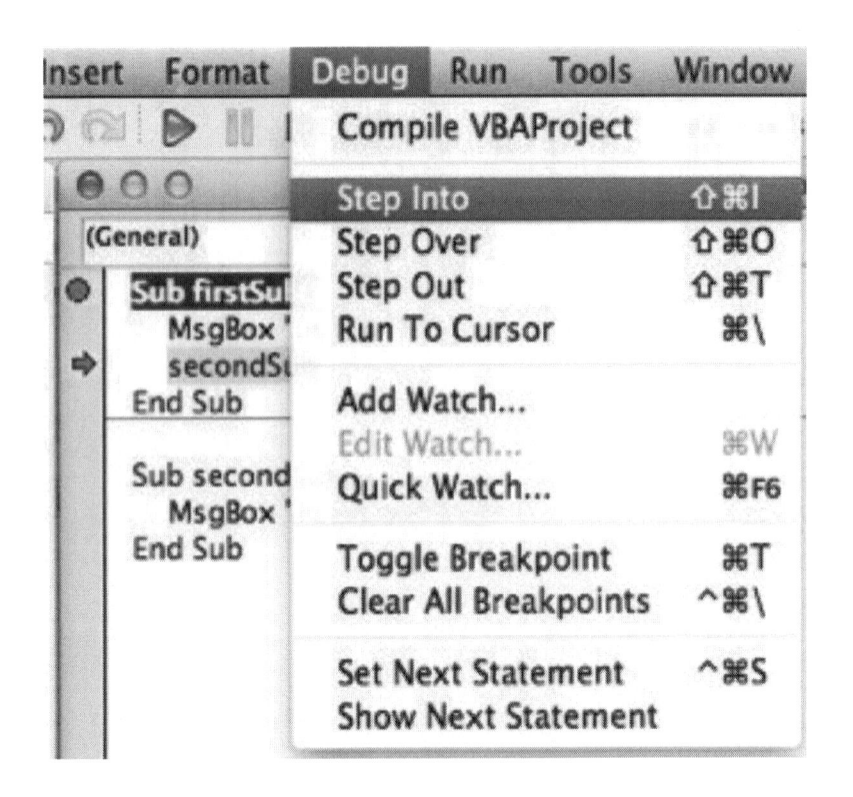

fig. 31

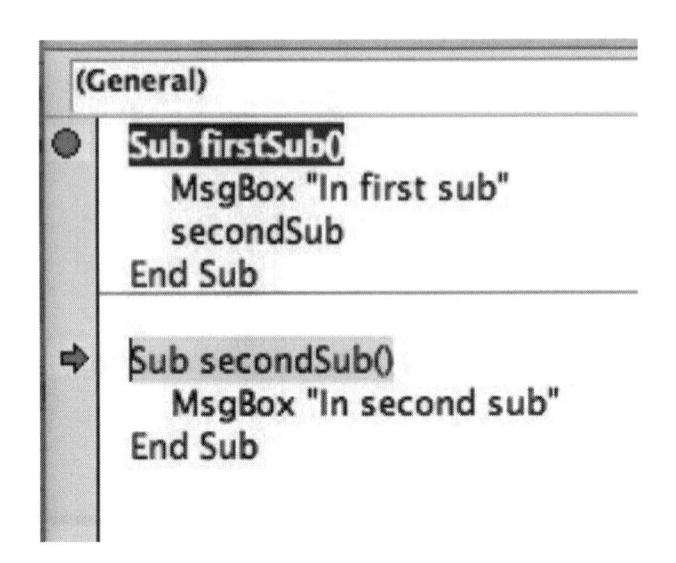

fig. 31b

You have learned how to use the debugging function in particular, setting break points, stepping over and stepping into. Do note that you do not have to necessarily step over or step into all lines of code. For example, you can set two break points in your code and skip execution from the first break point to the next break point by pressing the 'Run' button.

30

In Summary

The debugging function is a powerful tool to resolve bugs as you build larger and more complex spreadsheets. Experiment with it and you will be largely rewarded!

Chapter 7: Using Worksheet Functions

You probably have used Excel worksheet functions like Sum(), Average(), Count() before. You can also use them in VBA code as well! To do so, you use the **Application.WorksheetFunction**.

```
Sub useFunction()
    Dim answer As Double

    myRange = Worksheets("Sheet1").Range("A1:A10")
    answer = Application.WorksheetFunction.Sum(myRange)
    MsgBox answer
End Sub
```

Code 25 - WorksheetFunction Sum

Figure 25 illustrates the sum of the Application.WorksheetFunction to sum cells A1 to A10.
The below code is first used to define the range to sum.
myRange = Worksheets("Sheet1").Range("A1:A10")
We define if by specifying the worksheet, *Worksheets("Sheet1")*, and then its range *Range("A1:A10")*. We then assign this range to the variable *myRange*.

We next provide *myRange* to the *Application.WorksheetFunction.sum(<range>)* function which will sum up the value of the cells in that range. We assign the computed result to the variable *answer*.

Finally, we output *answer* in a message box.

Commonly used Financial Functions

While not exhaustive, we provide a list of commonly used functions in Excel.

ACCRINT:
Returns the accrued interest for a security that pays periodic interest
DB:
Returns the depreciation of an asset for a specified period by using the fixed-declining balance method
DDB:
Returns the depreciation of an asset for a specified period by using the double-declining balance method or some other method that you specify
FVSCHEDULE:
Returns the future value of an initial principal after applying a series of compound interest rates
IRR:

Returns the internal rate of return for a series of cash flows

PMT:

Returns the periodic payment for an annuity

PV:

Returns the present value of an investment

TBILLPRICE:

Returns the price per $100 face value for a Treasury bill

TBILLYIELD:

Returns the yield for a Treasury bill

YIELD:

Returns the yield on a security that pays periodic interest

YIELDDISC:

Returns the annual yield for a discounted security; for example, a Treasury bill

YIELDMAT:

Returns the annual yield of a security that pays interest at maturity

Common Statistical Functions

AVERAGE

Returns the average of its arguments

CONFIDENCE

Returns the confidence interval for a population mean

COUNT

Counts how many numbers are in the list of arguments

COUNTIF

Counts the number of nonblank cells within a range that meet the given criteria

GEOMEAN

Returns the geometric mean

POISSON

Returns the Poisson distribution

STDEV

Estimates standard deviation based on a sample

TDIST

Returns the Student's t-distribution

VAR

Estimates variance based on a sample

ZTEST

Returns the one-tailed probability-value of a z-test

Common Math, Trigonometry Functions

ABS

Returns the absolute value of a number

CEILING
Rounds a number to the nearest integer or to the nearest multiple of significance

COS
Returns the cosine of a number

COSH
Returns the hyperbolic cosine of a number

DEGREES
Converts radians to degrees

EVEN
Rounds a number up to the nearest even integer

EXP
Returns *e* raised to the power of a given number

FACT
Returns the factorial of a number

FLOOR
Rounds a number down, toward zero

GCD
Returns the greatest common divisor

LCM
Returns the least common multiple

LN
Returns the natural logarithm of a number

LOG10
Returns the base-10 logarithm of a number

PI
Returns the value of pi

POWER
Returns the result of a number raised to a power

PRODUCT
Multiplies its arguments

QUOTIENT
Returns the integer portion of a division

RADIANS
Converts degrees to radians

RAND
Returns a random number between 0 and 1

RANDBETWEEN
Returns a random number between the numbers you specify

SIN
Returns the sine of the given angle

SINH
Returns the hyperbolic sine of a number

SQRT
Returns a positive square root

SUBTOTAL
Returns a subtotal in a list or database

SUM
Adds its arguments

SUMIF
Adds the cells specified by a given criteria

SUMPRODUCT
Returns the sum of the products of corresponding array components

SUMSQ
Returns the sum of the squares of the arguments

TAN
Returns the tangent of a number

TANH
Returns the hyperbolic tangent of a number

TRUNC
Truncates a number to an integer

Common Text Functions

CONCATENATE
Joins several text items into one text item

DOLLAR
Converts a number to text, using the $ (dollar) currency format

LEFT, LEFTB
Returns the leftmost characters from a text value

LEN, LENB
Returns the number of characters in a text string

LOWER
Converts text to lowercase

MID, MIDB
Returns a specific number of characters from a text string starting at the position you specify

RIGHT, RIGHTB
Returns the rightmost characters from a text value

T
Converts its arguments to text

TEXT
Formats a number and converts it to text

TRIM
Removes spaces from text

UPPER
Converts text to uppercase

VALUE
Converts a text argument to a number

Chapter 8: Referring and Operating on Things in Excel

To refer to a workbook
Workbooks("Book1.xls")

To refer to a worksheet
Workbooks("Sheet1") or *Sheets("Sheet1")*

To refer to a cell
Range("A1") or *Cells(1,5)*

To refer to a range
Range("A1:C5") or *Range("RangeName")*

To refer to several cells
Range("A1,C5,D3") or *Range("A1:C5,D3,E3:F4")*

To refer to a column
Columns("D:D")

To refer to a row
Rows(6)

To refer to multiple rows
Rows("6:50")

To refer to multiple rows with variable row numbers
Rows(startRow &":" & endRow)

To refer to the 4th row of a range
Range("A1:C5").Rows(4)

To refer to all the cells in a worksheet
Worksheets("Sheet1").Cells

To refer to the current selected object (cell, range, etc.)
Selection

To refer to the current active workbook
ThisWorkbook

To refer to the current active cell
ActiveCell

Activate a worksheet
Sheets("Sheet1").Activate

Select all the cells in the active worksheet
Cells.Select

Selecting a Range
Range("A1:C5").Select

Clear the current Selection
Selection.Clear

Delete rows
Rows("5:10").Delete

Delete columns
Columns("1:5").Delete

Activate a worksheet
Sheets("Sheet1").Activate

Copy and pasting a Range
Range("A1:C5").CopyRange("D1")

Insert a row before row 3
Rows(3).Insert

Insert a sheet before the active sheet
Sheets.Add or *Worksheets.Add*

Delete a worksheet
Worksheets("Sheet1").Delete

Chapter 9: Recording Macros

Macros in Excel are actually VBA code that represent the actions we want to do or have done. So far, we have manual coded VBA to solve problems but do you know that whenever we perform an action in Excel, we can record these actions in VBA code as well?

This is extremely useful as we can take these recorded VBA code and perform repetitive actions with it. For example, populating a list of fields in a new sheet. We will illustrate recording a macro.

Record a macro by going to **View > Macros > Record Macro...**

Name the macro as 'Absolute' and click 'Ok' (Figure 81).

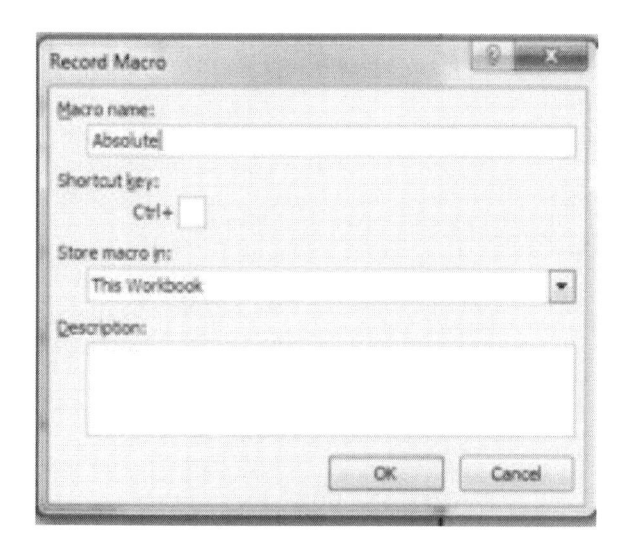

Figure 81 - Record Macro

In a sheet, type 'First Name' in cell A1, 'Last Name' in cell B1, 'Address' in cell C1. Click back on cell A1 (Figure 82).

Figure 82 - Recording of Macro

Stop recording of the macro by going to **View > Macros > Stop Macro...**

Congratulations, you have just recorded your first macro! Now let's put this macro to work.

Clear all data which you have previously entered in the sheet. Now click on Macros. Select our previously recorded macro 'Absolute' and click 'Run' (Figure 83).

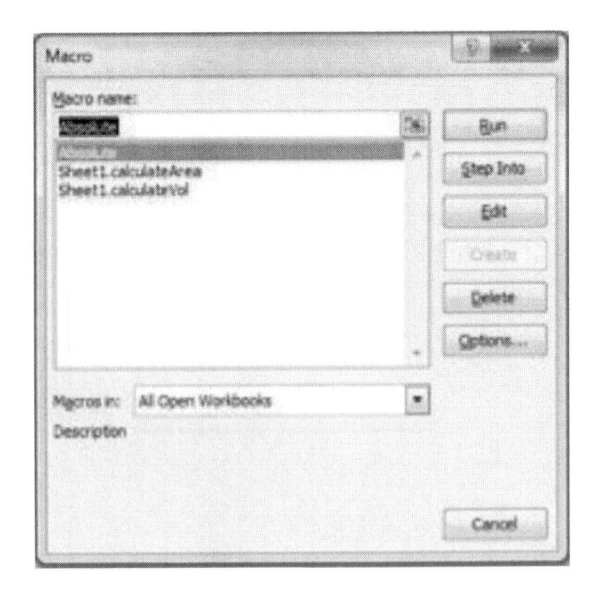

Figure 83 - Run Macro

Notice that 'First Name', 'Last Name', 'Address' appears in the first row again!

Macros can save us repetitive work. For example, if you want more fields to appear in the first row of a worksheet, you can extend this macro!

To view the VBA code of this macro, go the VBA editor by pressing 'Alt-F11' and click on Module 1.

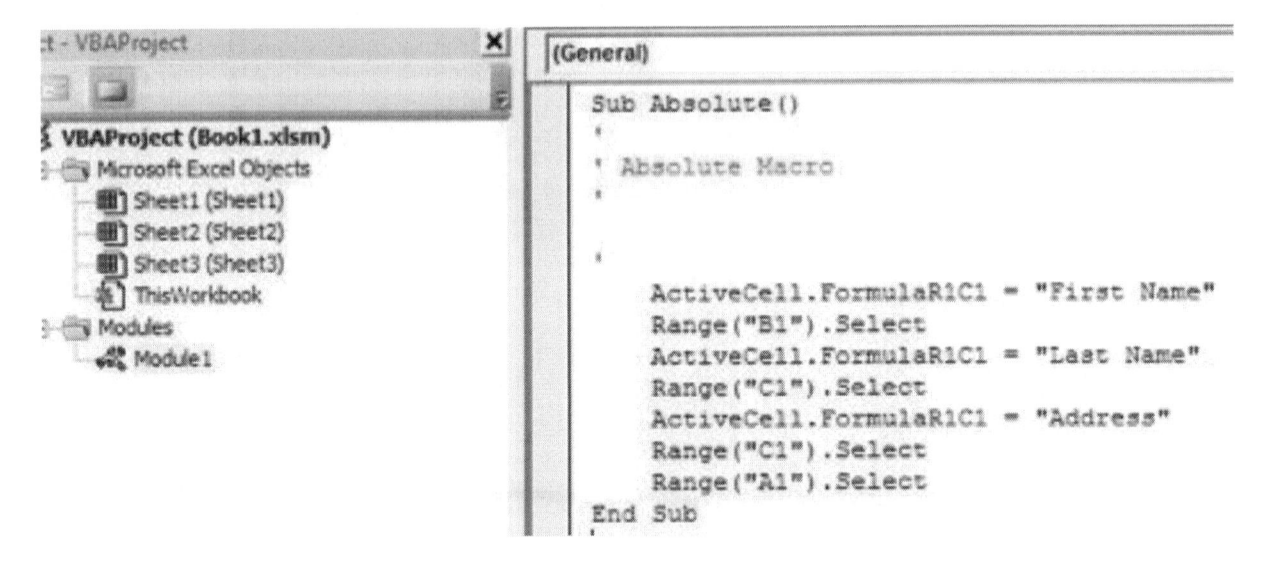

Figure 84 - VBA code of the Macro

However though, note that the fields always appear in the first row no matter where you run the macro. This is because the macro is recorded in the 'Absolute' mode. If you want the headers to appear starting from the current active cell, we have to record the macro in 'Relative' mode.

First click on '**Use Relative References**' in the macros button.

40

Now in a new sheet, re-record the previous macro of 'First Name', 'Last Name', 'Address' as you have done before. Name the macro as 'Relative'. Once done, click on any cell and run the 'Relative' macro. Notice that the 'First Name', 'Last Name', 'Address' values appear from the active cell now!

```
Sub Relative()
'
' Relative Macro
'

    ActiveCell.FormulaR1C1 = "First Name"
    ActiveCell.Offset(0, 1).Range("A1").Select
    ActiveCell.FormulaR1C1 = "Last Name"
    ActiveCell.Offset(0, 1).Range("A1").Select
    ActiveCell.FormulaR1C1 = "Address"
    ActiveCell.Offset(0, -2).Range("A1").Select
End Sub
```

Figure 85 - VBA code of 'Relative' macro

Figure 85 shows the VBA code of the 'Relative' macro. Notice the differences between the absolute and relative methods of recording macros.

Absolute Method:
Range("B1").Select
ActiveCell.FormulaR1C1 = "Last Name"

Relative Method:
ActiveCell.Offset(0, 1).Range("A1").Select
ActiveCell.FormulaR1C1 = "Last Name"

In the absolute method, there is an absolute reference to cell B1. In the relative method, there is a relative offset from the previous active cell.

Macro Code Generation in Real Time

We have seen the powerful code generated by recording macros. To truly see the code generation in real time, place Excel and the VBA editor one top of the other (Figure 86).

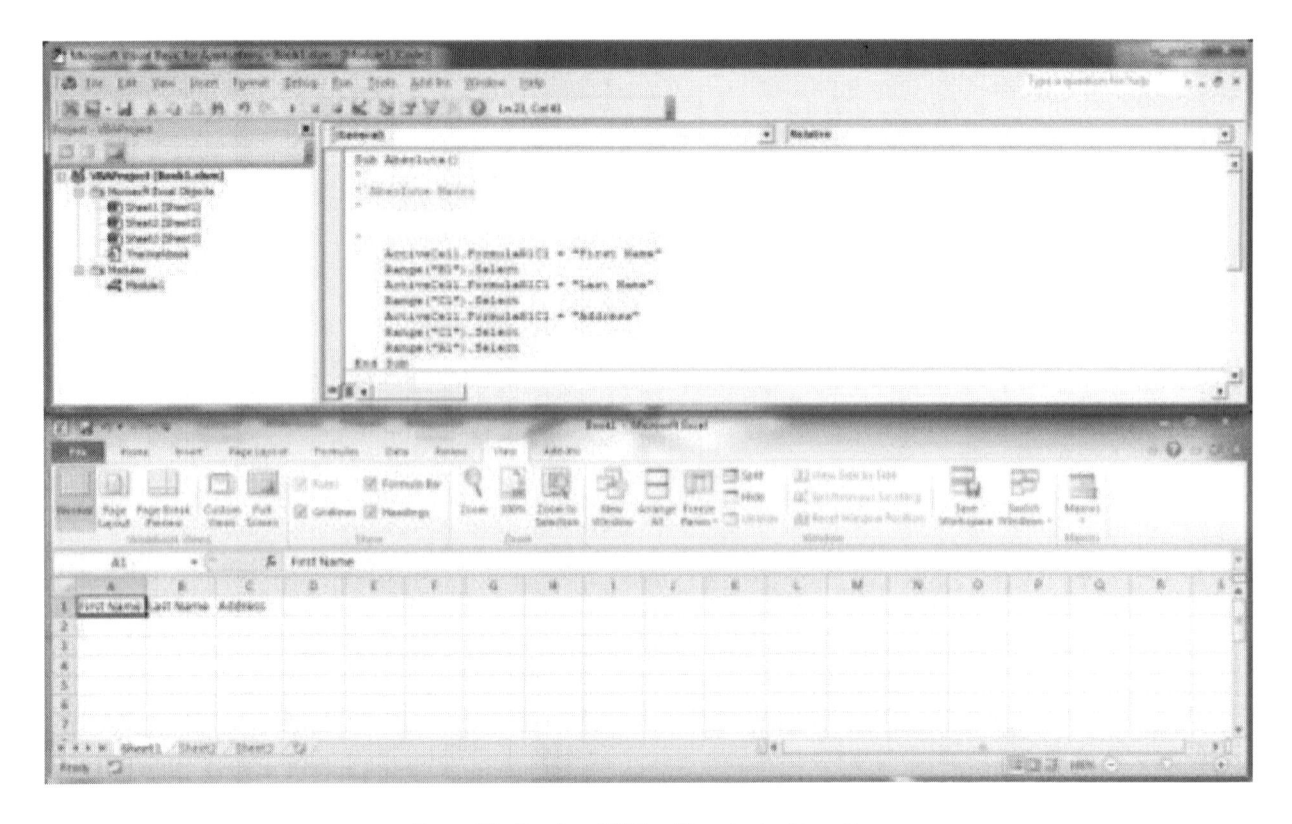

Figure 86 - Excel and VBA editor stacked together

In this setup, record a new macro and just do anything you want! You can see the VBA code being generated as you perform your actions in Excel, be it changing fonts, charts, vlookups etc!

Chapter 10: Creating User Forms

We have so far manually added data into our spreadsheet the conventional way, i.e. entering data into cells. We can use **Forms** to input data too. This is useful when data in excel sheets get too cluttered and user does not know where to enter what. A Form looks professional too!

Figure 91 shows a Form for users to enter stock data into a spreadsheet. Its fields are 'Company', 'Ticker code' and current Stock price. A user makes use of the Form to enter data into the worksheet instead of entering it directly.

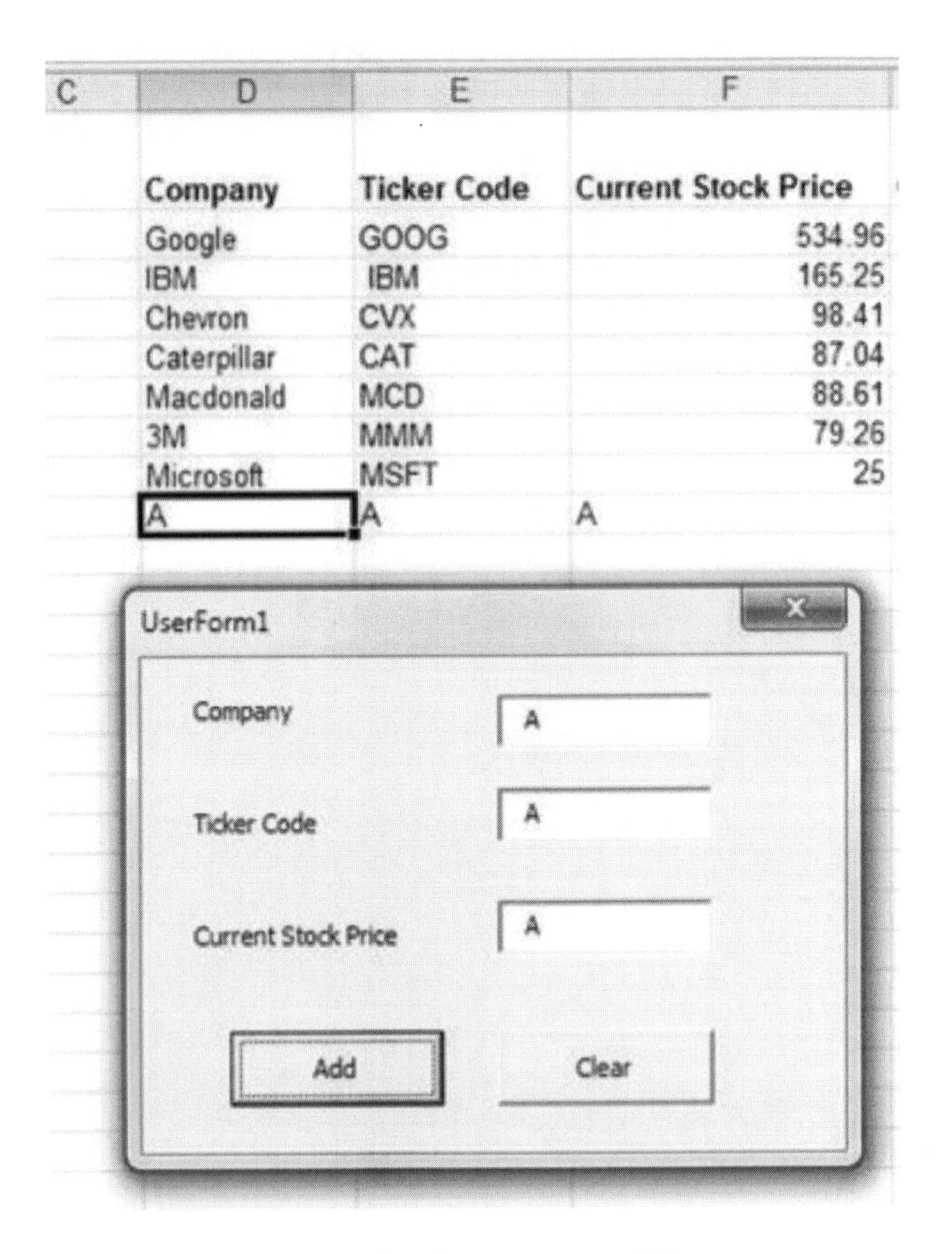

Figure 91 - A Form for user to enter stock data

To create a Form, open the VBA Editor by pressing Alt+F11.
Select **VBAProject** and click **'Insert' > 'UserForm'**. A Form should appear in the editor. (Figure 92).

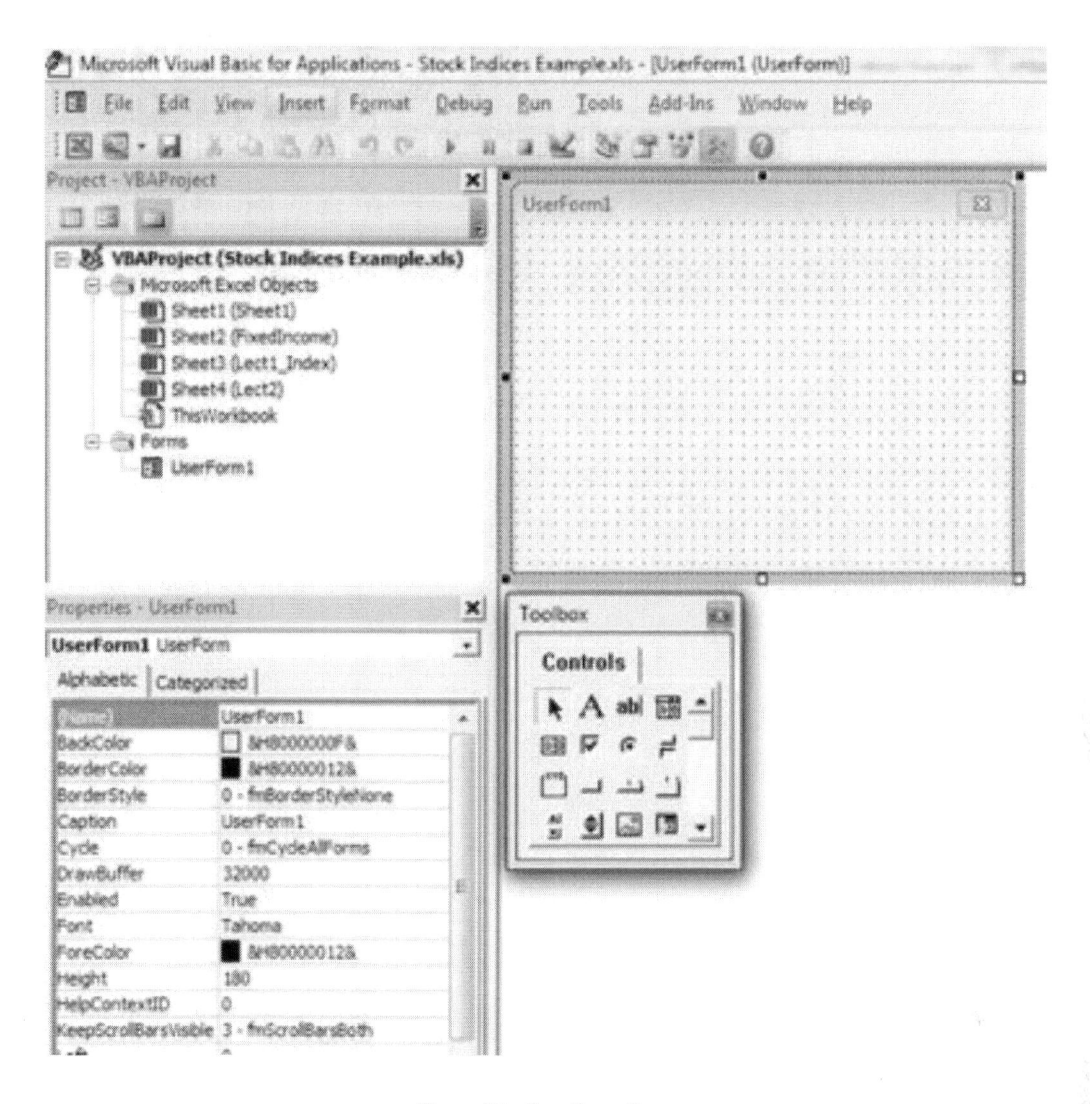

Figure 92 - Creating a Form

We are going to create a simple form to allow user to input *Company, Ticker Code* and *Current Stock Price* (Figure 93). Once you know the basic steps of creating a Form, you can go on and add more fields in the Form on your own.

D	E	F
Company	Ticker Code	Current Stock Price
Google	GOOG	534.96
IBM	IBM	165.25
Chevron	CVX	98.41
Caterpillar	CAT	87.04
Macdonald	MCD	88.61
3M	MMM	79.26
Microsoft	MSFT	25

Figure 93 - worksheet Data

First, drag a label from the toolbox into the Form (Figure 94). The toolbox contains User Interface (UI) Controls which we can drag and use in our forms.

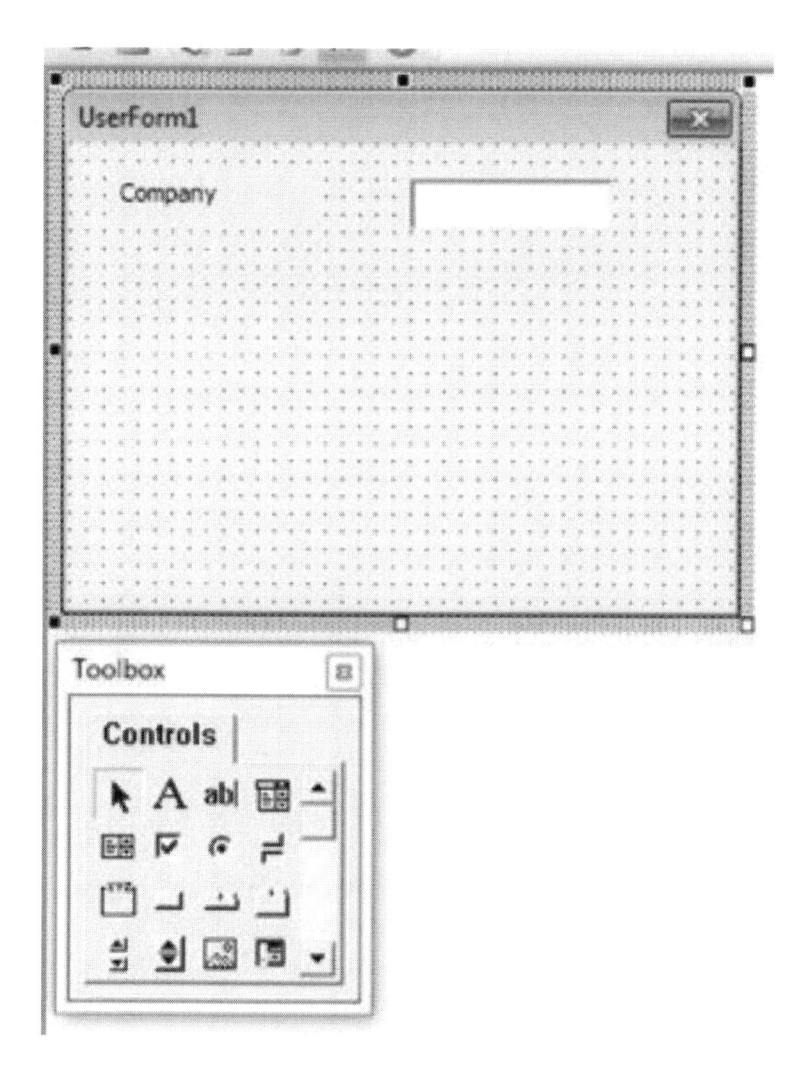

Figure 94 - Dragging UI Controls from the Toolbox

Change the caption of the label to *'Company'* by changing the **'Caption'** property in the properties window (Figure 95). Note that this applies to other UI Controls. You can change the appearing text via the Caption property.

47

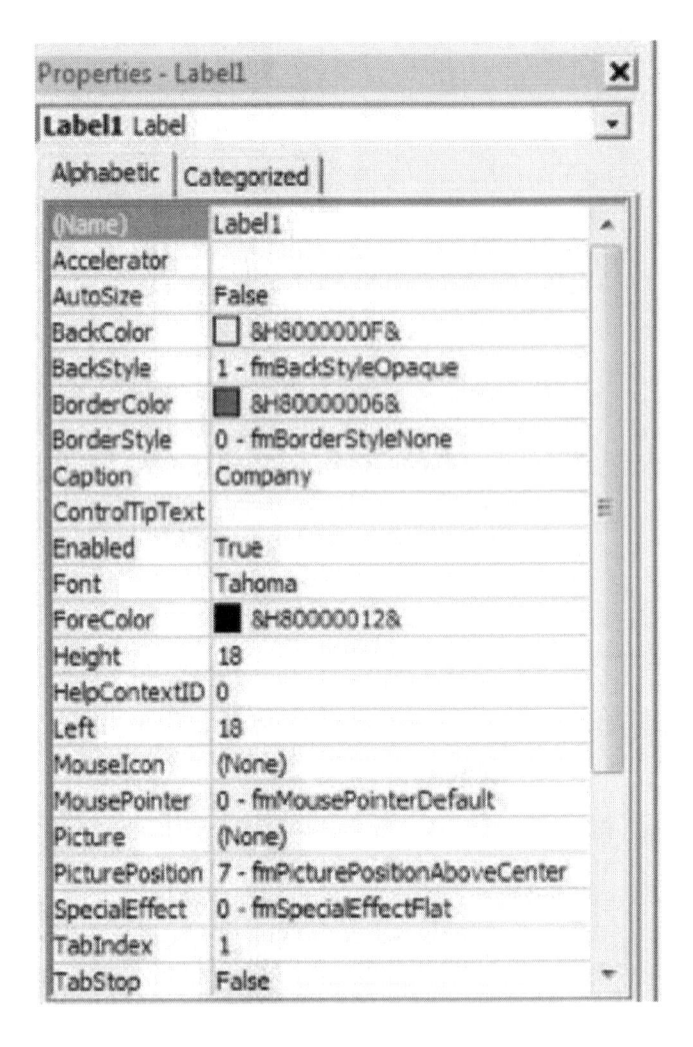

Figure 95 - Property Window

Next, drag a textbox into the Form (Figure 96).

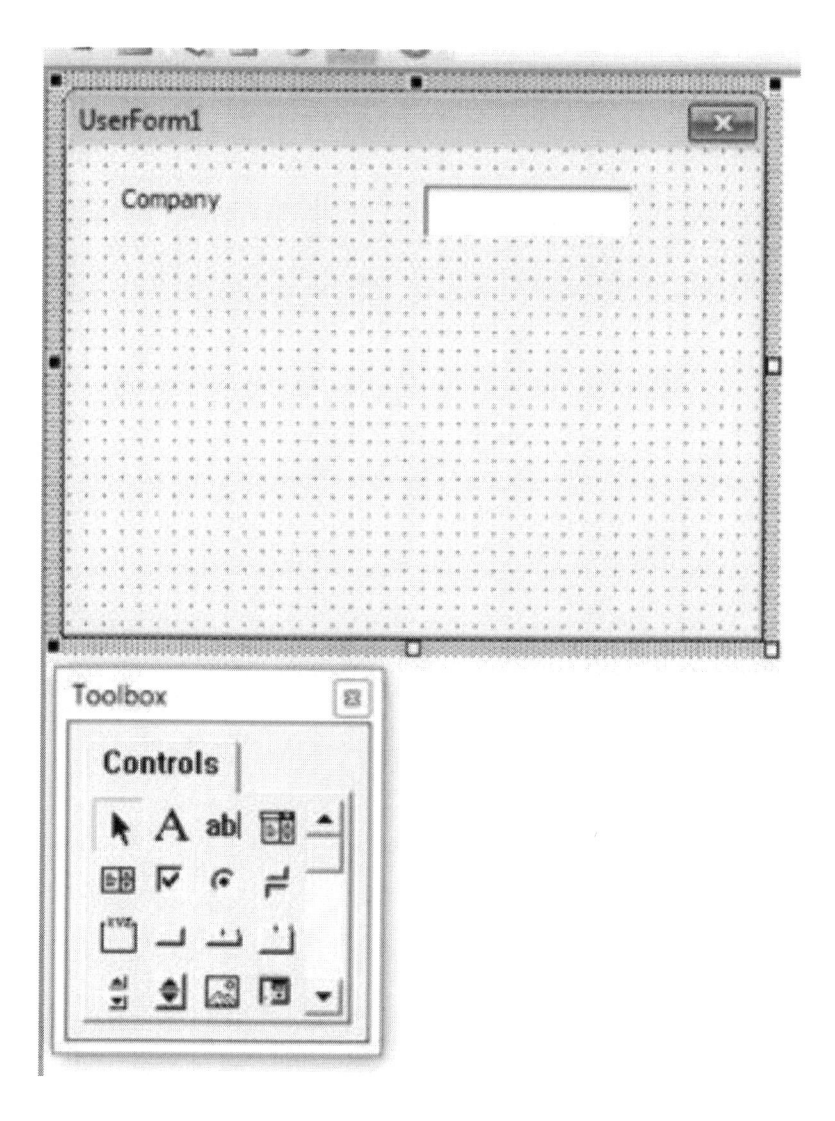

Figure 96 - Dragging a textbox from the Toolbox into the Form

Do the same for *Ticker Code* and *Current Stock Price* till your Form resembles that of in figure 97.

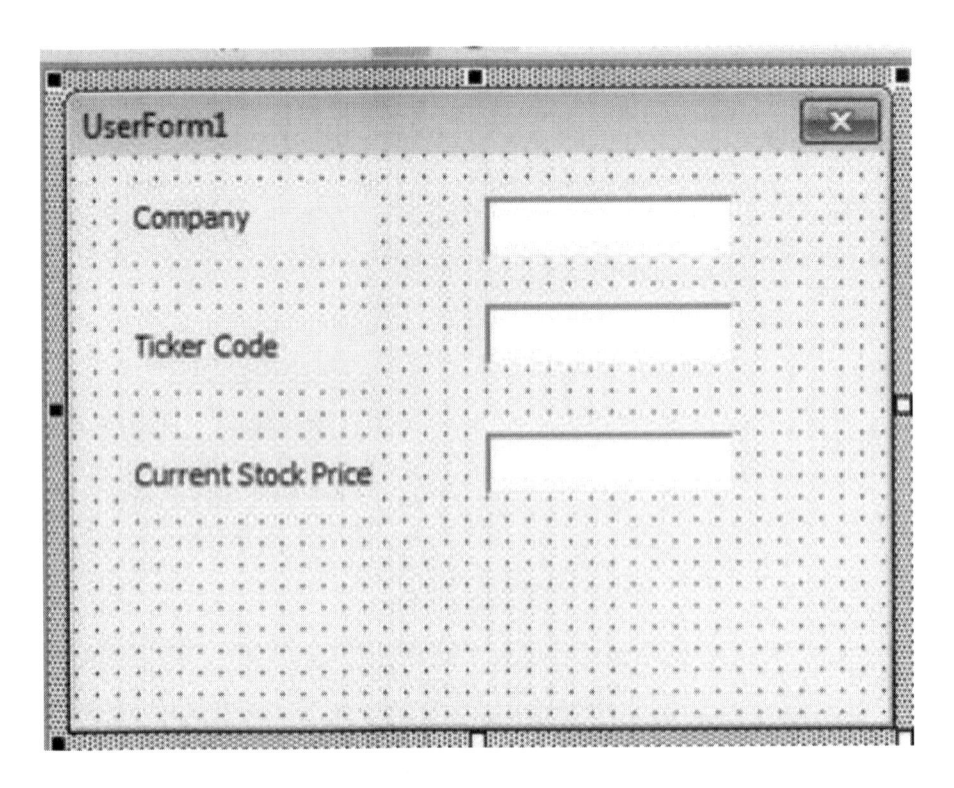

Figure 97

Press **F5** and you should see the Form displayed (Figure 98). You can type in texts in the textboxes but at this point in time, nothing works as we have not implemented the VBA code for the Form to work.

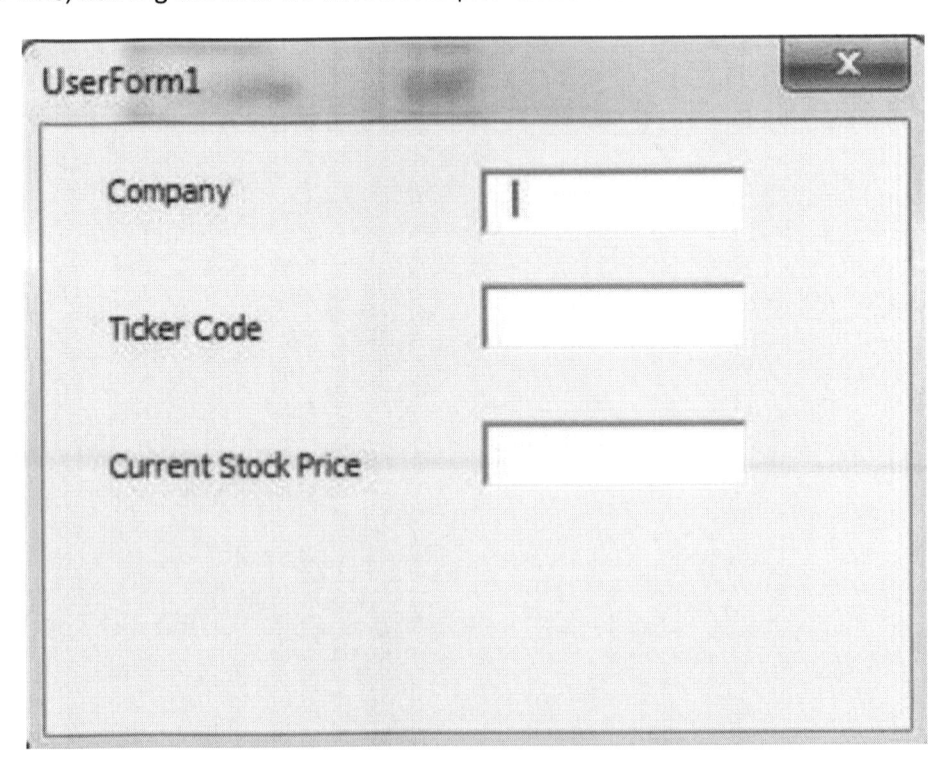

Figure 98

Before we go on, change the name property of each of the textboxes to *tbxCompany*, *tbxTickerCode* and *tbxStockPrice* (Figure 99).

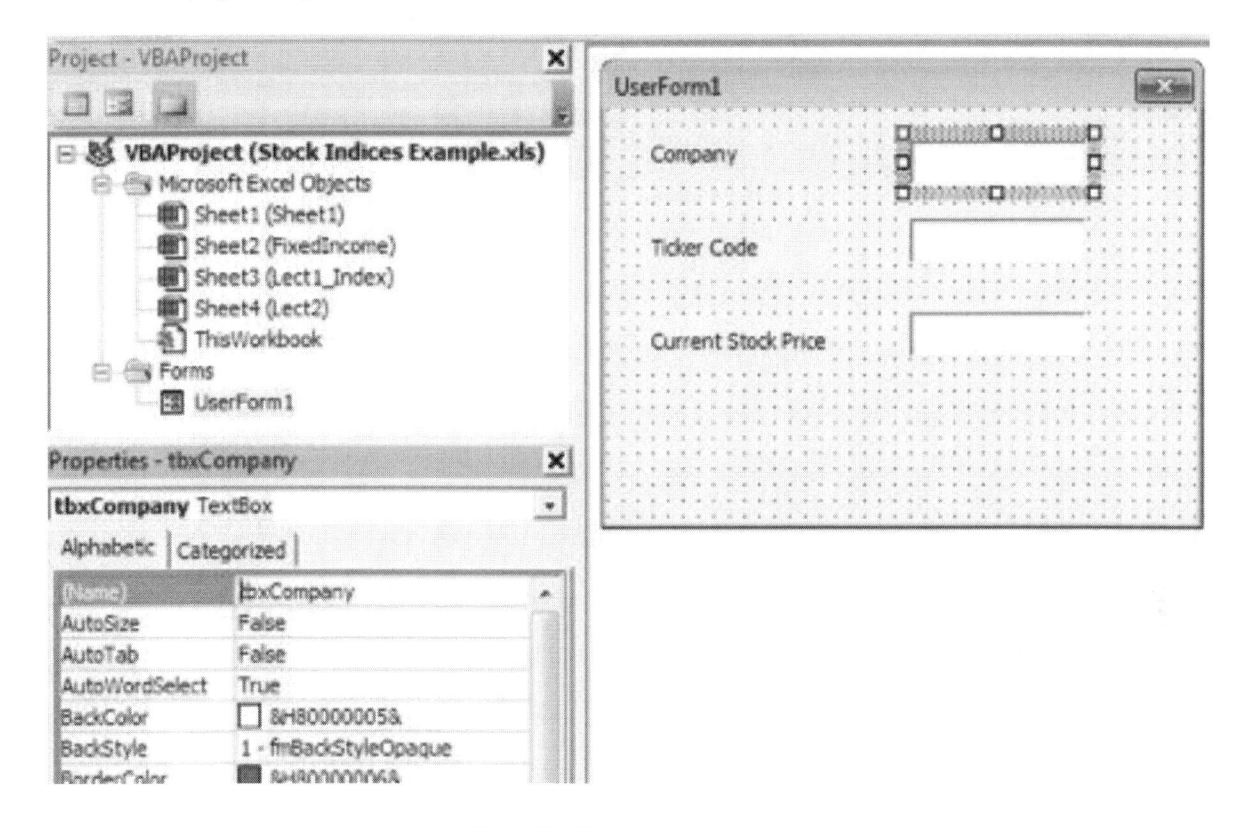

Figure 99 - Change name property

It is good practice to change the name property of the UI controls as later on in our VBA code, we will not be confused as to which UI Control we are referring to.

Adding Buttons

Next, drag and drop two command buttons on to the Form from the toolbox (Figure 99a).

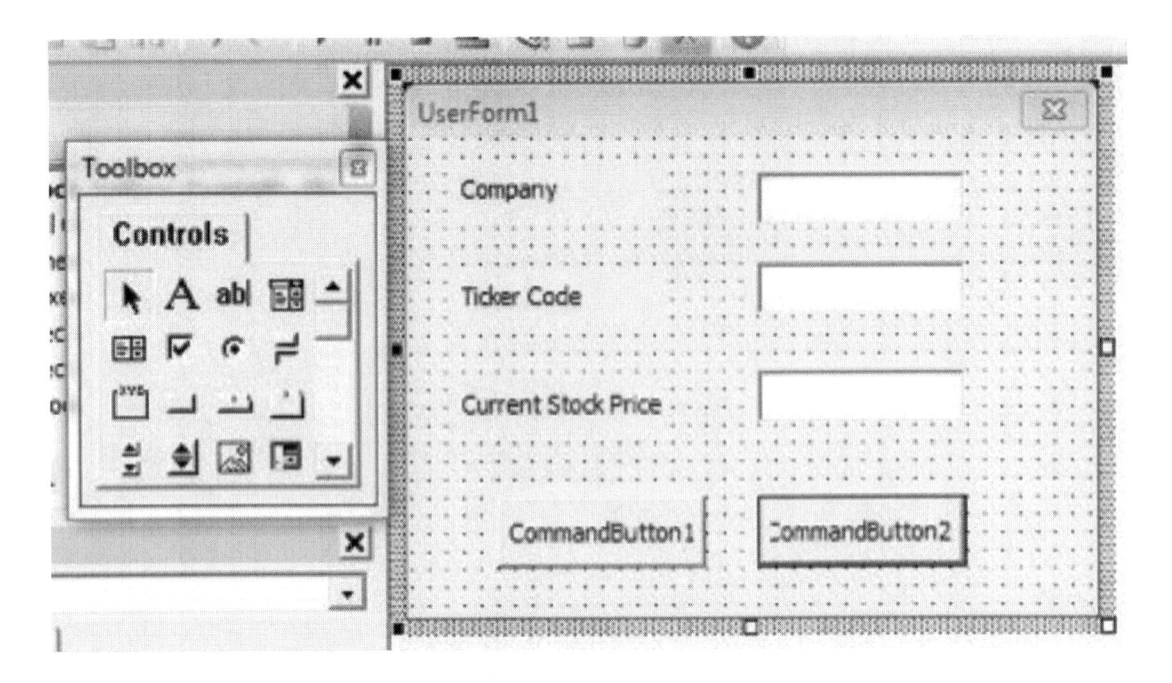

Figure 99a - Adding Buttons to the Form

Change the names of the buttons to *btnAdd* and *btnClear* (Figure 99b).
Change the caption of the buttons to *Add* and *Clear*.

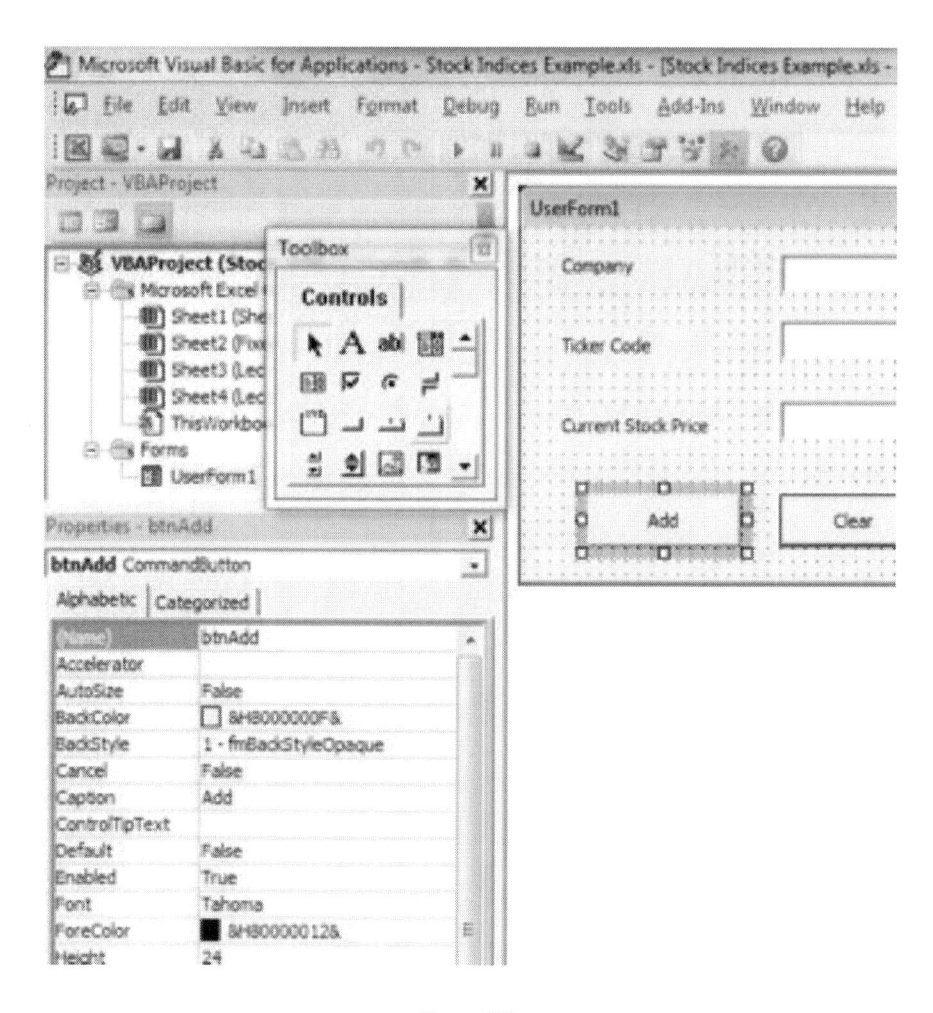

Figure 99b

Implementing the Button's Event Handler

Double click on the *Add* button. You should see a **Sub Routine** being created in the code editor (Figure 99c).

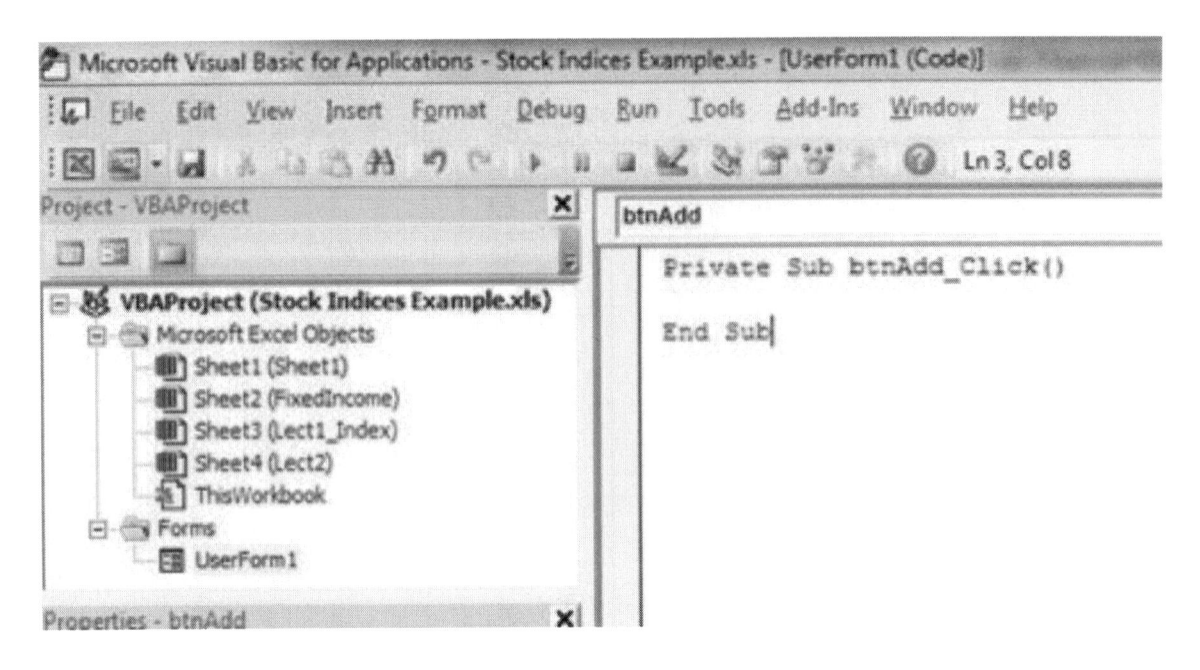

Figure 99c – Sub Routine btnAdd_Click

What we have created is a Sub Routine called **btnAdd-Click()** that is called when the user clicks on the Add button. This is also called an **Event-Handler**. *btnAdd-Click()* is a sub routine that handles the click event

Add the below text into the *btnAdd_Click()* sub routine (Figure 99d).

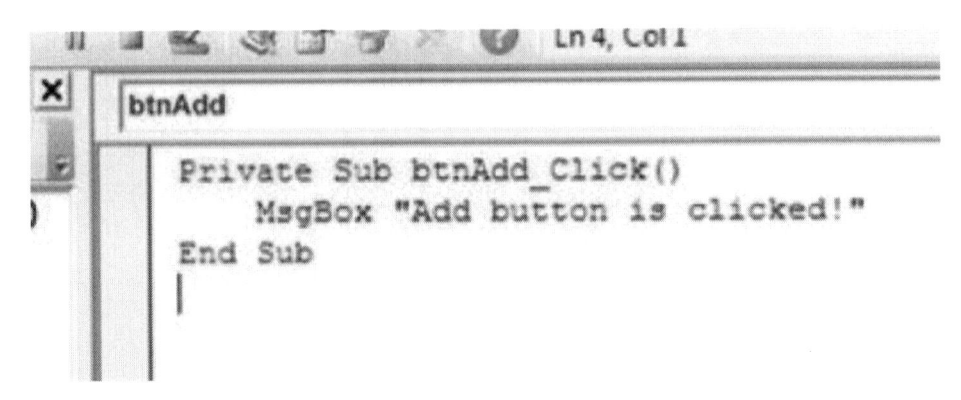

Figure 99d - Implementing the Sub-Routine

Run your Form by clicking on the green arrow.

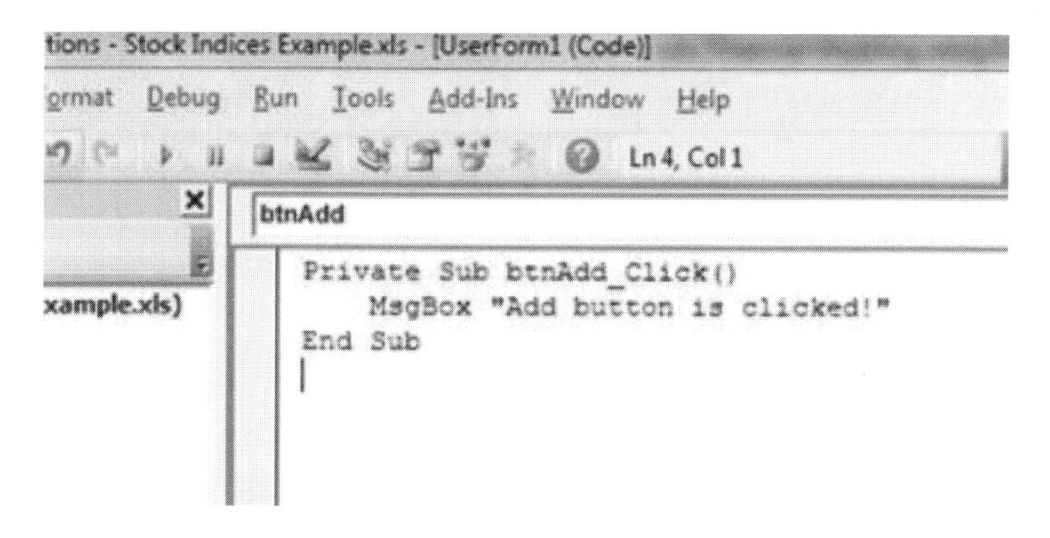

Figure 99e - Running the Form

Your Form will appear. Click on the *'Add'* button. A MessageBox will appear with the message we have entered earlier (Figure 99f).

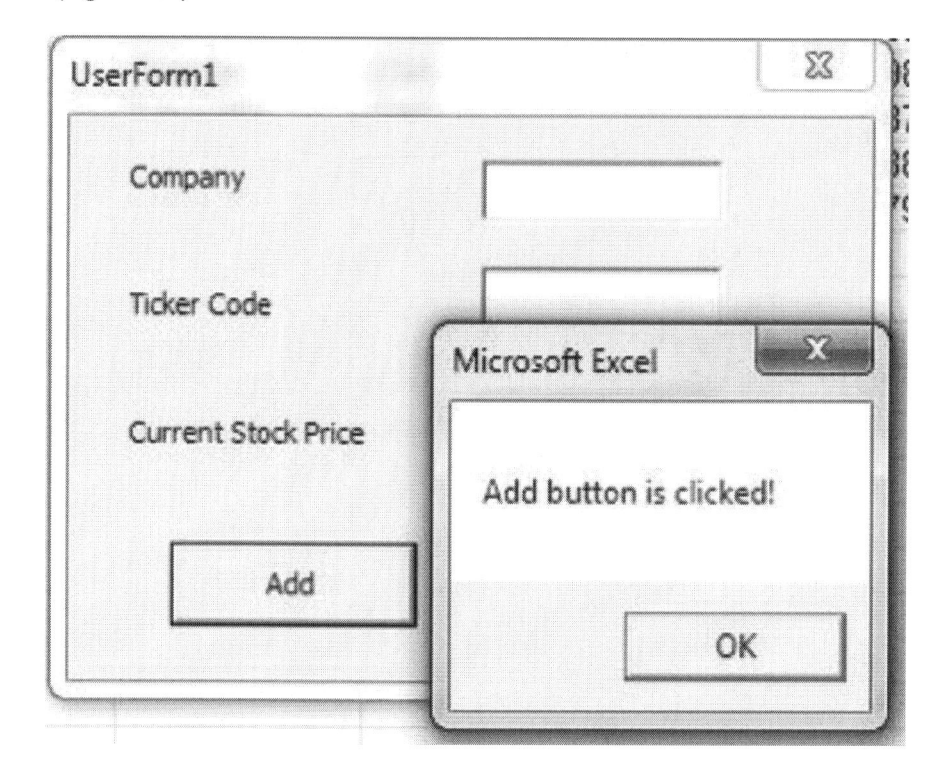

Figure 99f

This illustrates how a sub-routine can be called by clicking a button. Let's go on and add more code to implement our Form. Remember that the purpose of our Form is to allow adding of more Stocks into our spreadsheet.

55

Implementing the Form

We will first implement the 'Clear' button. The clear button resets all the textboxes of the Form. Create the click subroutine of *btnClear* by double clicking on the *Clear* button similar to the Add button. Fill in the codes below into the subroutine.

Private Sub btnClear_Click()
  tbxCompany.Text = ""
  tbxTickerCode.Text = ""
  tbxStockPrice.Text = ""
End Sub

Try running your Form again. Enter in values into each of the text boxes. Click on the 'Clear' button. Notice that all the text boxes' values are cleared. This is because for each of the textboxes, we have set the **text property** of each textbox to "", a blank value.

We next implement the *Add* button. Fill in the codes in figure 99g into the *btnAdd_Click* subroutine. We will explain the code in the next few pages.

```
Private Sub btnAdd_Click()
    rowCounter = 2
    While Cells(rowCounter, 1).Value <> ""
        rowCounter = rowCounter + 1
    Wend

    Cells(rowCounter, 1).Value = tbxCompany.Text
    Cells(rowCounter, 2).Value = tbxTickerCode.Text
    Cells(rowCounter, 3).Value = tbxStockPrice.Text
End Sub
```

Figure 99g - Implementing the btnAdd_Click Subroutine

rowCounter = 2
rowCounter is a variable that will represent the current row of data. We set it to 2 because our data starts from row 2 (Figure 99h).

	A	B	C
1	Company	Ticker Code	Current Stock Price
2	Google	GOOG	300
3	IBM	IBM	200
4			

Figure 99h

When we add new stock info, we add it to the end of the list. Hence, we also need to know the row which is at the end. To do so, we need to iterate through each row till there a row where there is no more data.

To do so, we use a *While* loop, and compare the cell in row *rowCounter*, column 1 if it is blank. We use column 1 because column 1 is the column for company name.

While Cells(rowCounter, 1).Value <> ""
  rowCounter = rowCounter + 1
Wend

If company name is not blank, the condition will return true and we will continue iterating through the loop. The body of the loop causes *rowCounter* to increment by one. i.e., we go on to the next row of data.

When we finally exit the *While* loop, our current cell will be at a cell which has no data. Which means that it has reached the end of the list where we want it.

At that row, we add the new company stock info by assigning the text boxes values to the cells of that row in columns 1 (company), 2 (ticker code) and 3 (stock price).

Cells(rowCounter, 1).Value = tbxCompany.Text
Cells(rowCounter, 2).Value = tbxTickerCode.Text
Cells(rowCounter, 3).Value = tbxStockPrice.Text

Run the Form. Fill in values into the textboxes and click *Add*. A new row of data should appear (Figure 99i).

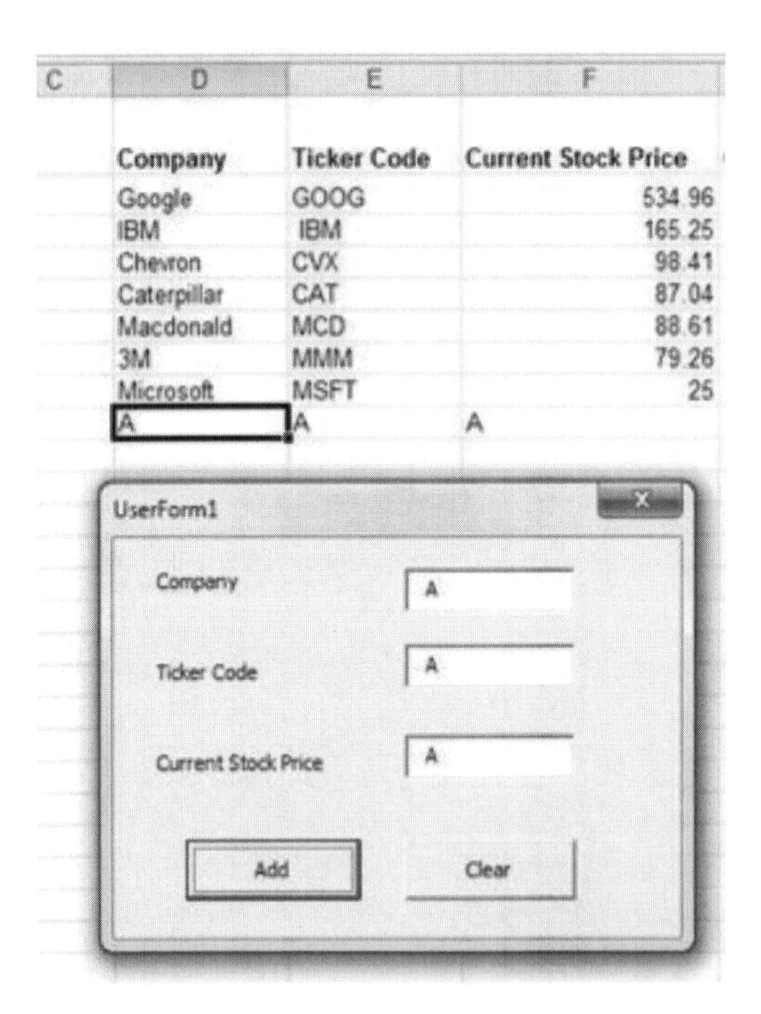

Figure 99i - Completed Form

Calling our Form

We have completed implementing the Form. But how do we call the Form from our spreadsheet besides going to the VBA editor?

Insert a 'Shape' into the worksheet by clicking on 'Insert', then choosing your shape (Figure 99j). I have chosen a circle for my example. This will act as a button to call the Form.

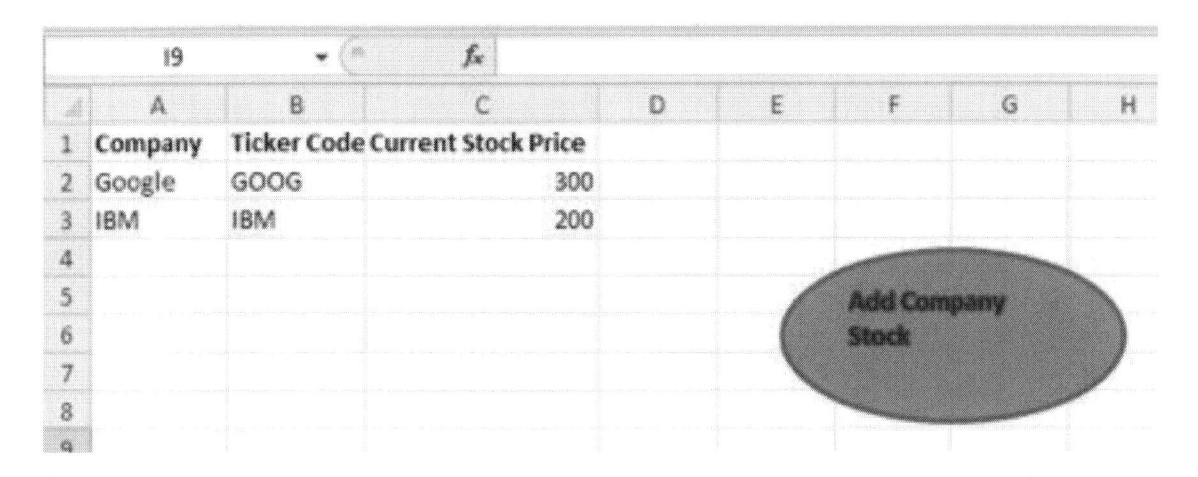

Figure 99j - Inserting a Shape

Right click on the shape, click on '**Assign Macro**'.
You should see a Form appearing similar to this one. We are trying to assign a Macro to this shape whenever a user clicks it. A Macro is a subroutine in Excel VBA.
Click on '**New**'.

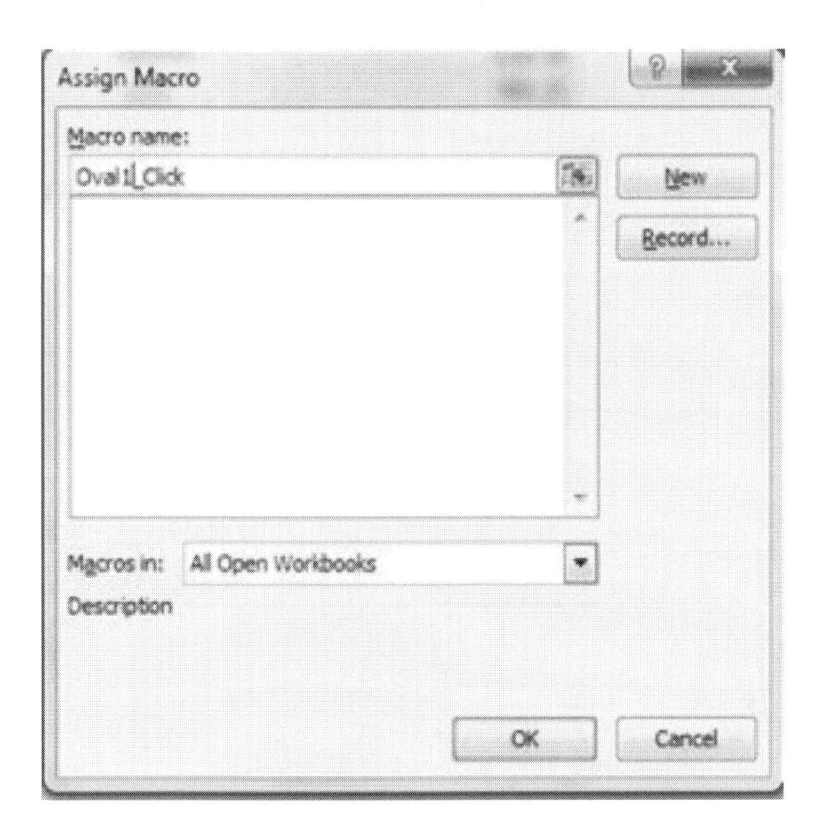

Figure 99k - Assign Macro

You should be brought to the VBA editor with a new sub routine created for you (Figure 99l). This is the sub routine that is called when a user clicks on the shape you created earlier. It is also an Event handler sub routine similar to the one we implemented for our buttons. In the same way, the shape acts as a button.

59

Figure 99l

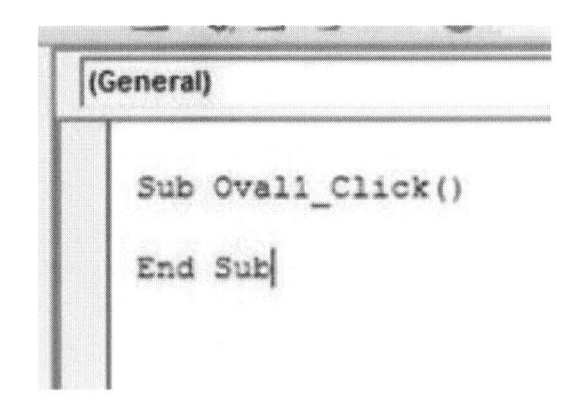

Fill in the code in bold into the sub routine.

Sub Oval1_Click()
   UserForm1.Show
End Sub

In the code, we are showing the Form to the user by calling the Show method of the Form called *UserForm1*
*Note that my *UserForm1* is just the name of the Form. You can name your Form any name just you can name your buttons, textboxes any name.

Go back to your worksheet and click on the newly created button. Your Form should now appear when you click on the button.

In Summary

You have learned how to create user forms in Excel vba and use it for accepting user input to the worksheet. You have learned how to use form controls like labels, textboxes and buttons in your form to direct the user where to enter what input. In the next chapter, we introduce more form controls.

Chapter 11: More User Form Controls

In this chapter, we will introduce more user controls to beef up your forms. In fig. 80, we have designed a Stock Purchase Form. Drag and drop the UI controls into your own form as per shown in the figure. Notably, the new UI controls introduced are the listbox, combo box, radio button, and picture frame.

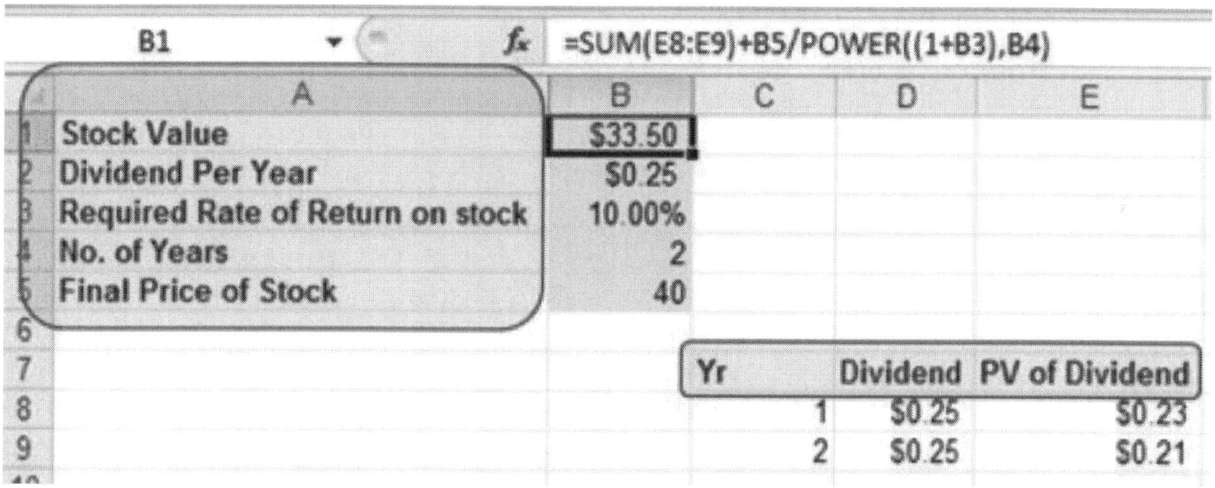

B1 =SUM(E8:E9)+B5/POWER((1+B3),B4)

	A	B	C	D	E
1	Stock Value	$33.50			
2	Dividend Per Year	$0.25			
3	Required Rate of Return on stock	10.00%			
4	No. of Years	2			
5	Final Price of Stock	40			
6					
7			Yr	Dividend	PV of Dividend
8			1	$0.25	$0.23
9			2	$0.25	$0.21

Fig. 80

When you run your form, it should like figure 81.

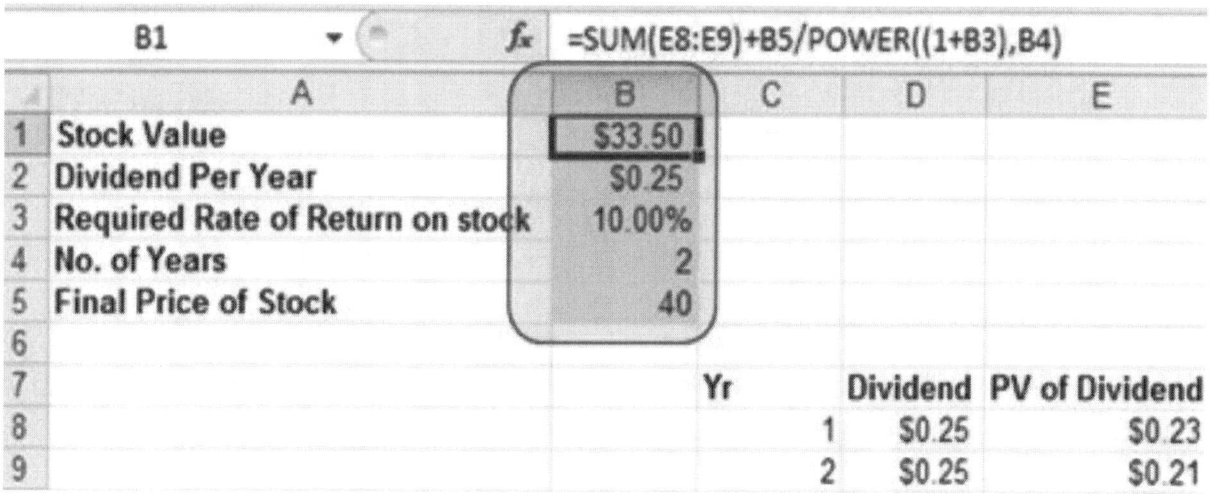

B1 =SUM(E8:E9)+B5/POWER((1+B3),B4)

	A	B	C	D	E
1	Stock Value	$33.50			
2	Dividend Per Year	$0.25			
3	Required Rate of Return on stock	10.00%			
4	No. of Years	2			
5	Final Price of Stock	40			
6					
7			Yr	Dividend	PV of Dividend
8			1	$0.25	$0.23
9			2	$0.25	$0.21

Fig. 81

The first thing we have to do is populate the listbox and combo box for which users can select the stock they want to order and the quantity. We first populate the values in a worksheet as in figure 82.

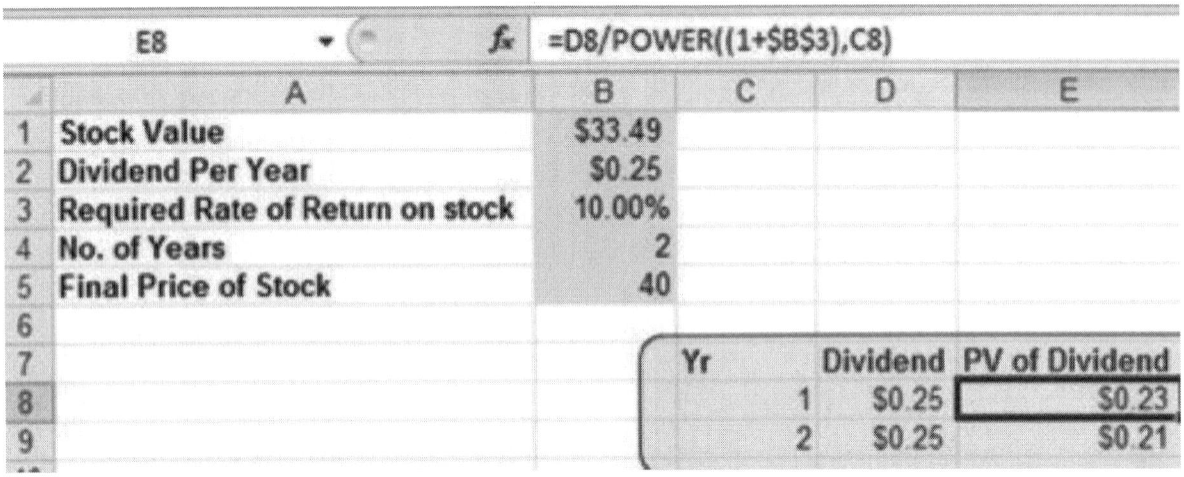

Fig. 82

Now, in the vba editor, select the UserForm, and select 'Initialize' from the right drop down box. A 'UserForm_Initialize' sub will be generated for you (fig. 83).

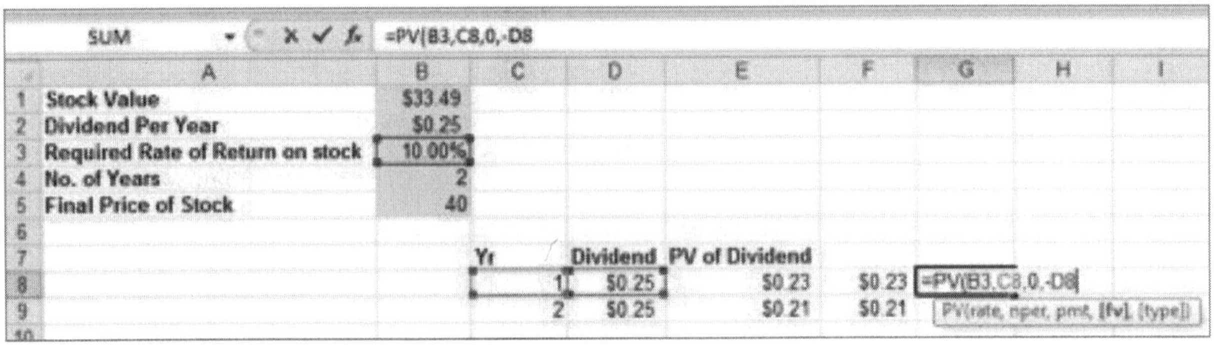

Fig. 83

This sub is called when the form first initializes, i.e. when it starts up. This is known as an event handler which handles events that occur. We will talk more about event handlers for workbooks and worksheets in another chapter.

Fill in the below codes in bold.

Private Sub UserForm_Initialize()

    Dim cell As Range

    For Each cell In Range("A2:A5")

        ListBox1.AddItem cell.Value

    Next cell

```
    For Each cell In Range("B2:B5")

        ComboBox1.AddItem cell.Value

    Next cell

End Sub
```

Now run the form again (fig. 84). This time, you should see the list box and combo box populated with values from your worksheet.

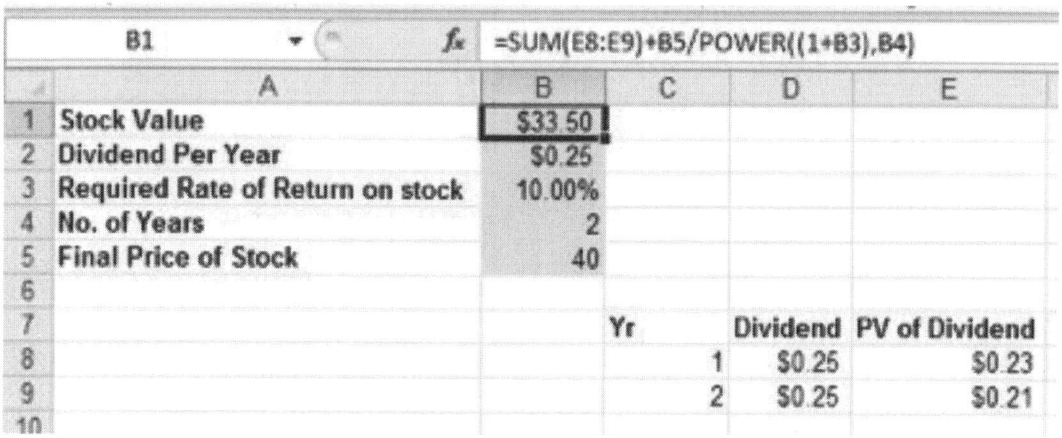

B1 =SUM(E8:E9)+B5/POWER((1+B3),B4)

	A	B	C	D	E
1	Stock Value	$33.50			
2	Dividend Per Year	$0.25			
3	Required Rate of Return on stock	10.00%			
4	No. of Years	2			
5	Final Price of Stock	40			
6					
7			Yr	Dividend	PV of Dividend
8			1	$0.25	$0.23
9			2	$0.25	$0.21
10					

Fig. 84

Code Explanation

What has happened was that we have placed two 'For each' loops in the initialize sub. The first loop (shown below) loops through the range A2:A5 and adds the value of each cell into the listbox1 with the 'AddItem' method of the list box.

```
Private Sub UserForm_Initialize()

    Dim cell As Range

    For Each cell In Range("A2:A5")

        ListBox1.AddItem cell.Value

    Next cell
```

The second loop does a similar thing only that it loops through the range of B2:B5 and adds its cell values into the combo box.

```
    For Each cell In Range("B2:B5")

        ComboBox1.AddItem cell.Value

    Next cell
```

End Sub

We next work on the radio buttons as I like to call it but Excel calls it an 'option button'. First, let's rename the radio buttons. Note that when i say rename, i mean renaming the name of the object and not its caption. This is necessary when i reference the object in vba code later on.

Rename the buy radio button to 'buyOptionButton' and the sell radio button to 'sellOptionButton' (fig. 85). Remember that you rename via the properties pane and edit the value of 'Name'.

```
Sub calculateDDM()
    Dim dividend As Double
    Dim reqdReturn As Double
    Dim numOfYears As Integer
    Dim finalStockPrice As Double
    Dim sumOfPV As Double

    'take user input
    dividend = Cells(2, 2).Value
    reqdReturn = Cells(3, 2).Value
    numOfYears = Cells(4, 2).Value
    finalStockPrice = Cells(5, 2).Value

    'Generate dividend payouts and output them to Excel Sheet
    rowCounter = 8
    For counter = 1 To numOfYears
        Cells(rowCounter, 3).Value = counter
        Cells(rowCounter, 4).Value = dividend
        Cells(rowCounter, 5).Value = Application.WorksheetFunction.PV(reqdReturn, counter, 0, -dividend)
        sumOfPV = sumOfPV + Cells(rowCounter, 5).Value
        rowCounter = rowCounter + 1
    Next counter

    'Output final calculated Stock Price
    sumOfPV = sumOfPV + Application.WorksheetFunction.PV(reqdReturn, numOfYears, 0, -finalStockPrice)
    Cells(1, 2).Value = sumOfPV

    MsgBox "DDM Calculation Complete!"
End Sub
```

Fig. 85

Next, double click on the command button to generate the 'CommandButton1_Click' event handler. This sub will be called when we click on the button. Fill in the below codes in bold.

Private Sub CommandButton1_Click()

    If buyOptionButton.Value Then

      MsgBox "Buy Order"

    Else

      MsgBox "Sell Order"

    End If

End Sub

Now run the macro (fig. 86). Click on the 'Sell' radio button. Notice that you can click on only either the 'buy' or 'sell' button but not both. This is the special characteristic of radio button unlike the checkbox which I will explain in a while.

A	B	C	D	E
Stock Value	$12.38			
Dividend Per Year	$0.25			
Required Rate of Return on stock	10.00%			
No. of Years	6			
Final Price of Stock	20			
		Yr	Dividend	PV of Dividend
		1	0.25	0.227272727
		2	0.25	0.20661157
		3	0.25	0.1878287
		4	0.25	0.170753364
		5	0.25	0.155230331
		6	0.25	0.141118483

Fig. 86

Click on the 'Place Order' button and you will see the MsgBox which indicates to you if you had clicked on the buy or sell radio button.

Code Explanation

When you click on the button, we use an If-Else statement to check if a radio button is checked. We do this with the below code.

If buyOptionButton.Value Then

If the buy radio button is checked, **buyOptionButton.Value** will return true. If its not checked, it will return false. Thus, if its checked, we proceed to output a message box of 'Buy Order'. Else, output 'Sell Order'.

```
Private Sub CommandButton1_Click()

    If buyOptionButton.Value Then

        MsgBox "Buy Order"

    Else

        MsgBox "Sell Order"

    End If

End Sub
```

Note that a **checkbox** works similar to a radio button. We can check if its checked using the .Value property value as well. What is different is that you can only check one radio button amongst multiple radio buttons but you can check multiple checkboxes in the same group.

Radio buttons are thus used for situations like specifying gender, i.e. either male or female where there is only one choice and checkboxes are used in examples like, where did you hear of us, friend, website, email, others etc. where you can select multiple choices.

To retrieve the values which the user has selected in the ListBox and Combobox, fill in the codes below.

Private Sub CommandButton1_Click()

   If buyOptionButton.Value Then

      MsgBox "Buy Order for " & ListBox1.Value & " Quantity: " & ComboBox1.Value

   Else

      MsgBox "Sell Order for " & ListBox1.Value & " Quantity: " & ComboBox1.Value

   End If

End Sub

Notice that we have concatenated the output string with ListBox1.Value and ComboBox1.Value. They respectively will return the user selected values of ListBox1 and ComboBox1. Thus, when you run the form, fill in the values, checked on the radio button and finally click on the 'Place Order' button, you will see the output as shown in figure 63.

```
Sub calculateDDM()
    Dim dividend As Double
    Dim reqdReturn As Double
    Dim numOfYears As Integer
    Dim finalStockPrice As Double
    Dim sumOfPV As Double

'take user input
dividend = Cells(2, 2).Value
reqdReturn = Cells(3, 2).Value
numOfYears = Cells(4, 2).Value
finalStockPrice = Cells(5, 2).Value
```

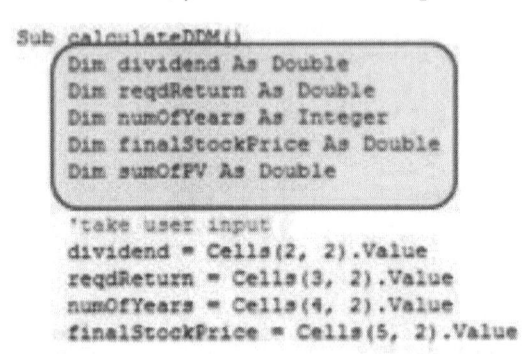

fig. 63

A sell order is correspondingly shown in fig. 64.

Notice that i have fill in the picture frame with a picture. You can easily do this by specifying an image file in the 'Picture' property of the frame.

```
Sub calculateDDM()
    Dim dividend As Double
    Dim reqdReturn As Double
    Dim numOfYears As Integer
    Dim finalStockPrice As Double
    Dim sumOfPV As Double

    'take user input
    dividend = Cells(2, 2).Value
    reqdReturn = Cells(3, 2).Value
    numOfYears = Cells(4, 2).Value
    finalStockPrice = Cells(5, 2).Value
```

fig. 64

In Summary

You have learned more controls in user forms. Experiment with other controls like tabs and frames. They can be used to beautify your form and many of them work in the same way!

Chapter 12: Using Event Handlers

There might be times when you want to call a macro when a particular event occurs. For example, if you are recording your stock portfolio in a worksheet, you might want to call a macro that changes cells with positive values green and cells with negative values in red every time a value of a cell changes. Another scenario is that you might want to clear a certain range of cells when you just open a workbook.

Using Worksheet Event Handlers

To do such related event based calling of macros, you can use event handlers. To start using them, in your vba editor, click on 'Sheet1' in the left pane under 'Microsoft Excel Objects' and select 'Worksheet' in the first drop down box on the right pane (fig. 61).

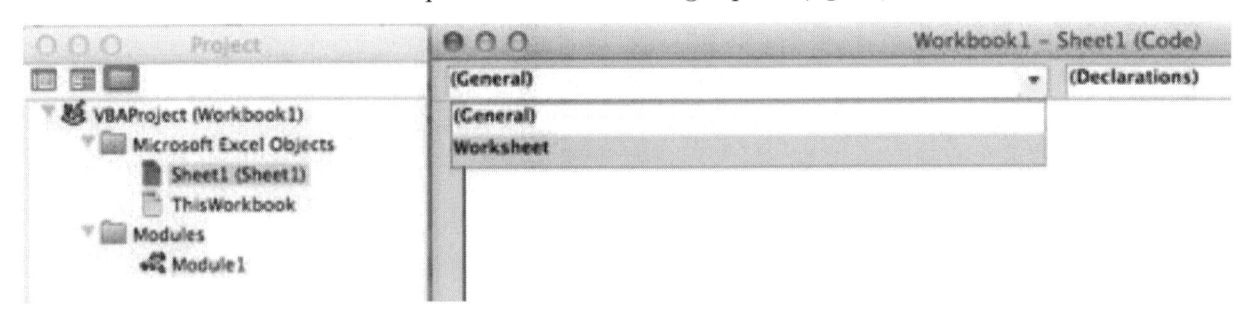

fig. 61

Click on the second drop down box to the right and you will see a list of event handlers (fig. 61b).

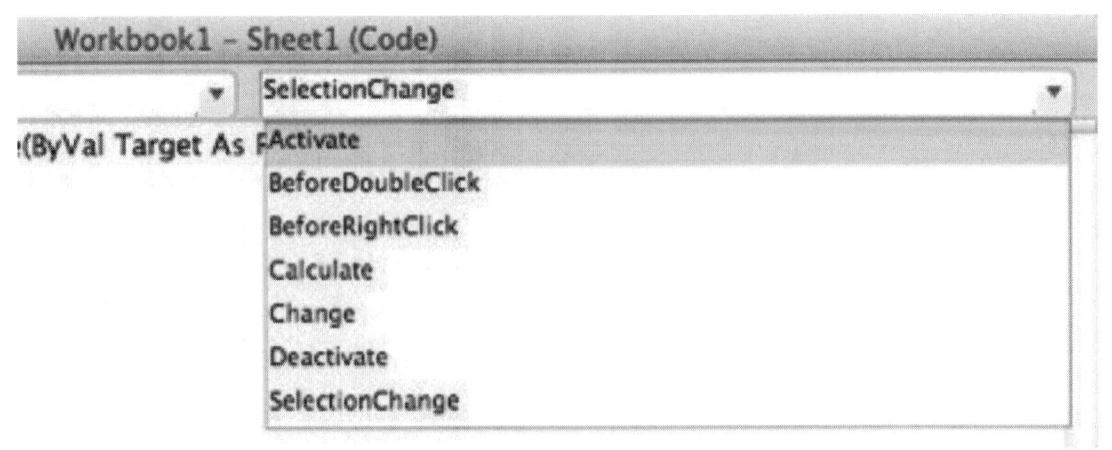

fig. 61b

Each of these event handlers correspond to handling an action that happens to the worksheet. To illustrate, click on 'Activate' in the drop down list. The below codes will be generated for you in the code editor.

Private Sub Worksheet_Activate()

End Sub

This sub routine will be called whenever the worksheet will be activated for e.g. if you switch to another sheet and switch back, the worksheet will be activated.

Fill in the below code in bold in the Worksheet_Activate subroutine.

Private Sub Worksheet_Activate()

MsgBox "Worksheet Activated"

End Sub

Try clicking on another sheet and back on to the original sheet. What do you see (fig. 62)?

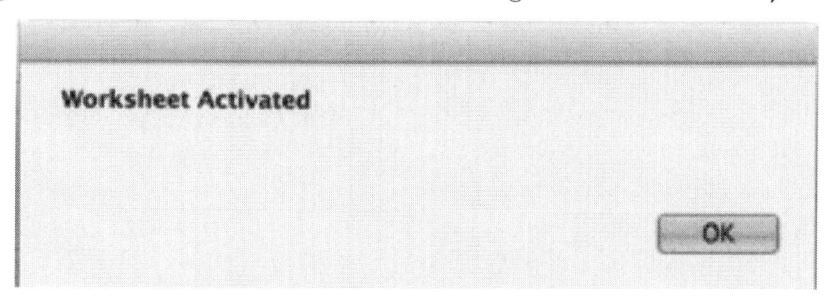

fig. 62

Thus, you can execute code that corresponds to whenever your worksheet is activated. You actually encountered previous event handlers when you implemented the click event handler of a button in a user form and also the form initialize event handler when the form first opens up and fills in values into the combo and list boxes.

There are several other worksheet event handler that you can use (fig. 63).

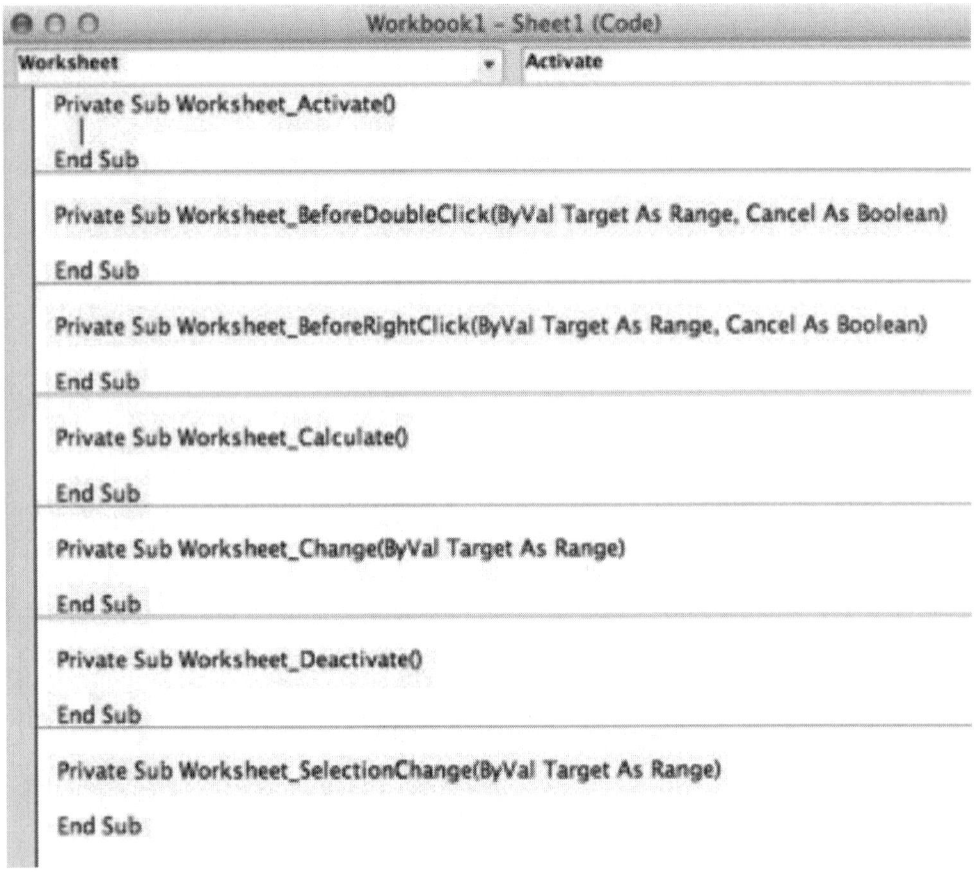

fig. 63

For example, the below Worksheet_Deactivate sub will be called when you switch away from the current sheet i.e. to deactivate it.

Private Sub Worksheet_Deactivate()

  MsgBox "Worksheet deactivate"

End Sub

Let's go on to a more useful example. Suppose you want to bold cells that you have selected. You can use the code below.

Private Sub Worksheet_SelectionChange(ByVal Target As Range)

  Dim cell As Range

  For Each cell In Target

    cell.Font.Bold = True

  Next cell

End Sub

What happens is that the 'SelectionChange' event handler is called when a selection of cells is changed. Furthermore, it provides the range of selected cells to the event handler. Thus in our code, we can use a 'For Each' loop to loop through the cells in the range and set each of them to having bold fonts.

The Worksheet_Change event handler is called when you change a value of a cell. Copy the following code into your editor. It prints out the cell address that has been changed as well as the new changed value in that cell.

Private Sub Worksheet_Change(ByVal Target As Range)

　MsgBox Target.Address & " has been changed to " & Target

End Sub

Now try changing a cell's value to '1234' and the 'Msgbox' in figure 64 will appear.

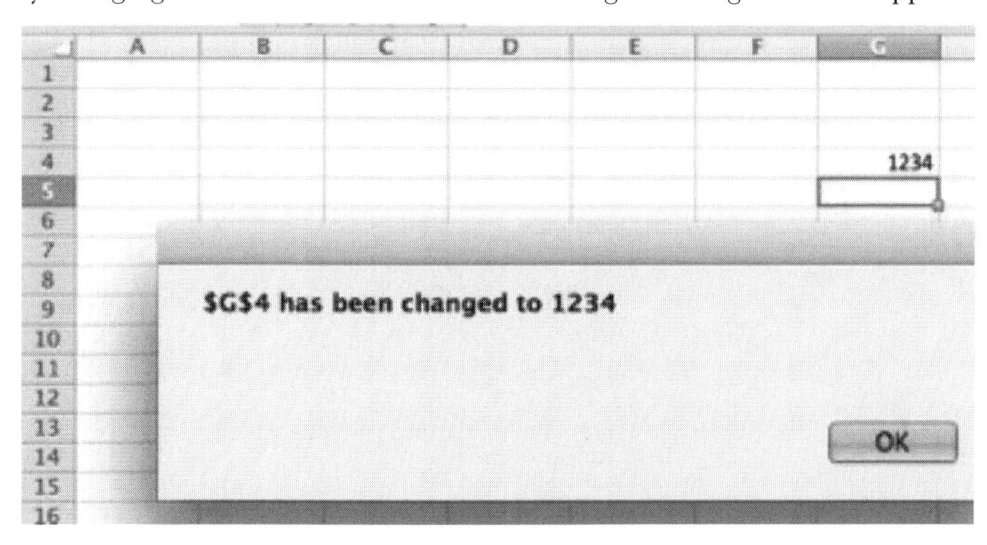

fig. 64

Let's go on to another event handler. The Worksheet_Calculate event handler is called when you key in a formula in to a cell such as '=sum' or '=1+1'.

Private Sub Worksheet_Calculate()

End Sub

There are also the 'BeforeDoubleClick' and 'BeforeRightClick' event handlers that by now should be self explanatory. I will leave the fun to you to experiment with them.

Using Workbook Event Handlers

We have gone through the worksheet based event handlers. There are also workbook based event handlers. What's the difference? Worksheet are individual sheets and their event handlers are based on each specific sheet. A workbook represents the entire excel file and thus will have event handlers like 'Open' (fig. 65), 'NewSheet', 'WindowResize'.

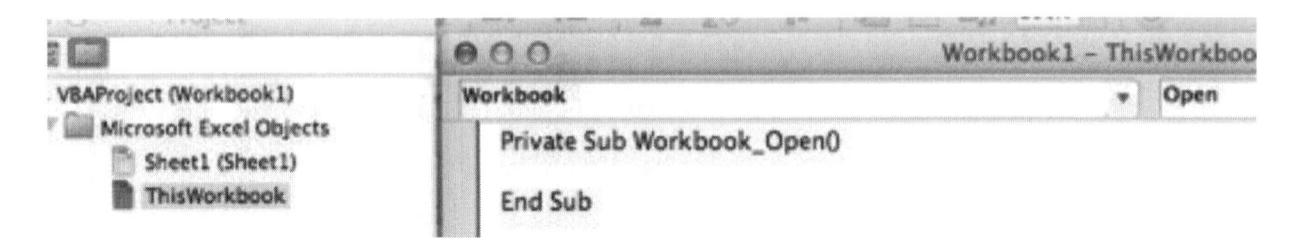

fig. 65

The workbook event handlers work the same way as the worksheet event handlers. For e.g. the Workbook_Open event handler is called when the workbook opens. One might re-initialize cells to certain default values when the workbook is first opened or extract data from a text file or website.

Fig. 65 shows more workbook event handlers.

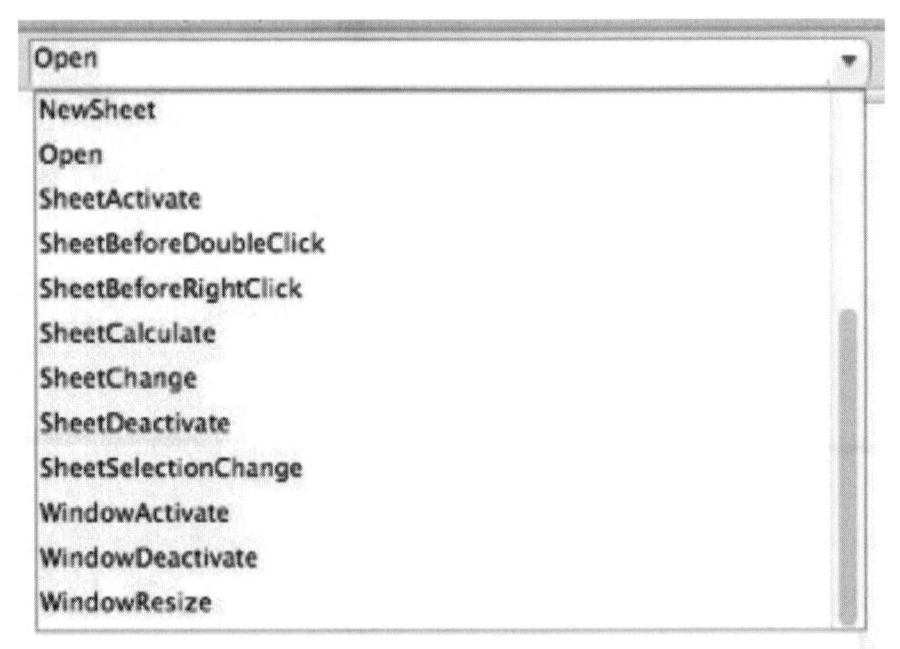

fig. 65

72

In Summary

You have learned how to implement event handlers for worksheets and workbooks. Try to integrate what you have learned from the very first chapter and create useful event handlers.

Chapter 13: Retrieving Data from the Web

Suppose i want to retrieve Facebook stock prices from Yahoo Finance into Excel (fig. 66). How can I do that with Excel VBA?

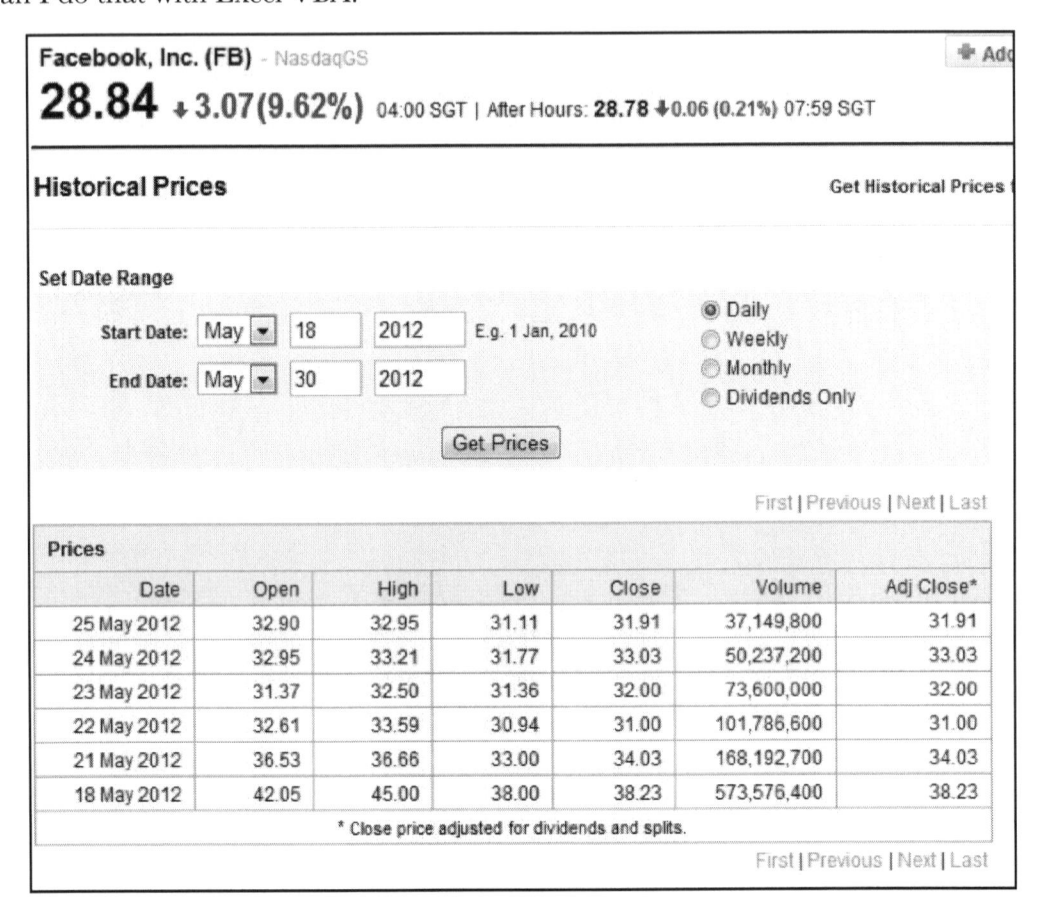

fig. 66

We will be using the 'Get Data from web function in excel'. We will generate the vba code for this by recording a macro.

Record a new macro and name it 'FBStockPrices' (fig. 66b).

74

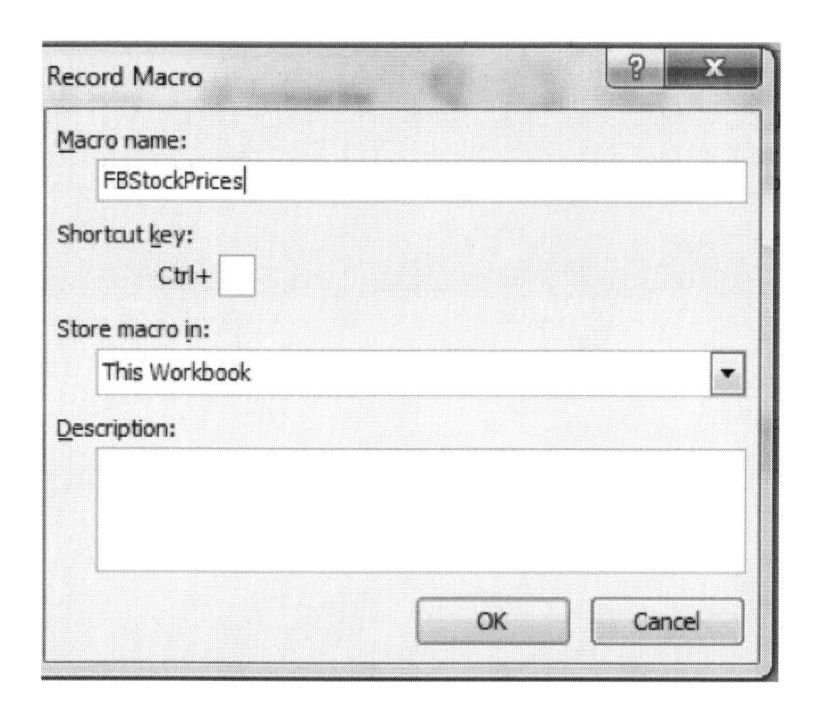

fig. 66b

With the macro recording going on, under 'Data', click on 'From Web' (fig. 67).

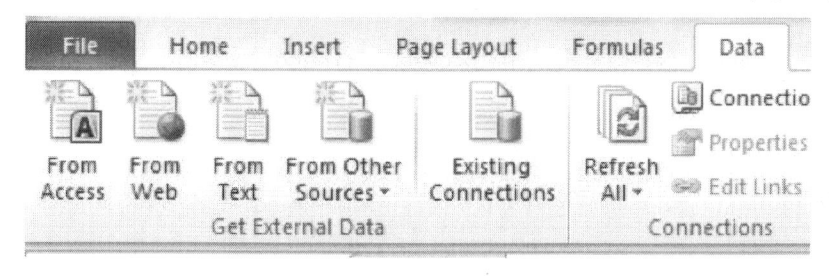

fig. 67

The 'New Web Query' form will appear (fig. 68). Under the 'Address' textbox, fill in the url which contains the stock prices of the stock. The web page should load and there should be arrows indicating the table that you want to extract.

75

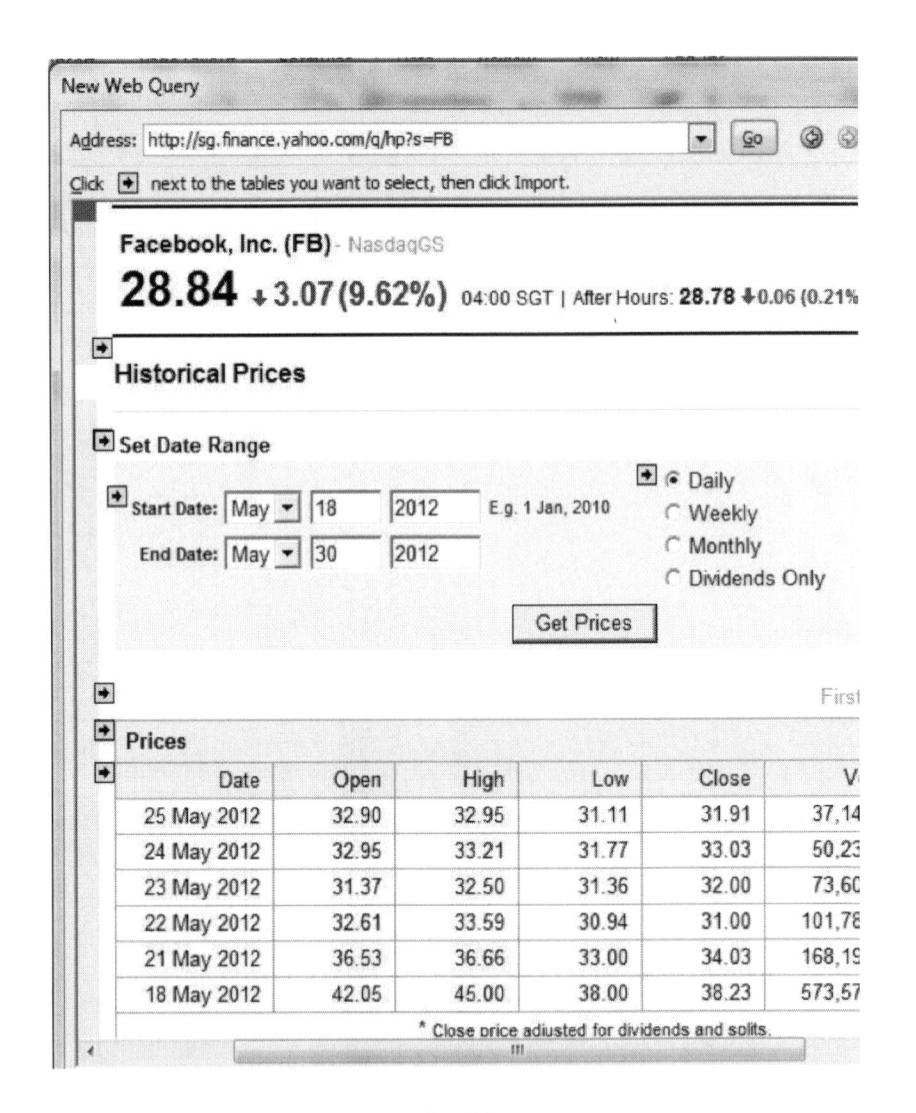

fig. 68

Choose the table with the stock prices (fig. 68b).

fig. 68b

Having selected the table, click on import. The 'Import Data' form will appear and ask where you want to put the data (fig. 69). Select Sheet1 A1 and click ok. The extraction will begin and after a few seconds of loading, the data should appear in your worksheet (fig. 69b).

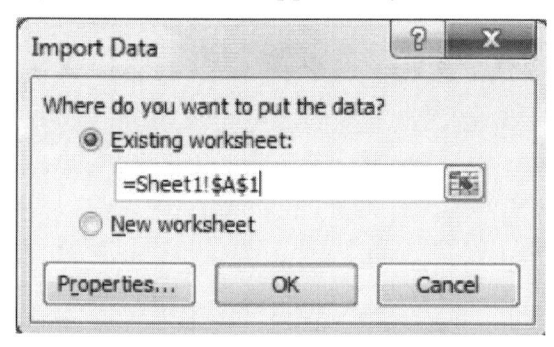

fig. 69

fig. 69b

At this point of time, you can stop recording the macro. In the vba editor, under modules, look at the code of the generated subroutine. A code sample is shown below.

Sub FBStockPrices()

' FBStockPrices Macro

   With ActiveSheet.QueryTables.Add(Connection:= _

      "URL;http://sg.finance.yahoo.com/q/hp?s=FB", Destination:=Range("$A$1"))

      .Name = "hp?s=FB"

      .FieldNames = True

      .RowNumbers = False

      .FillAdjacentFormulas = False

      .PreserveFormatting = True

```
.RefreshOnFileOpen = False

.BackgroundQuery = True

.RefreshStyle = xlInsertDeleteCells

.SavePassword = False

.SaveData = True

.AdjustColumnWidth = True

.RefreshPeriod = 0

.WebSelectionType = xlSpecifiedTables

.WebFormatting = xlWebFormattingNone

.WebTables = "15"

.WebPreFormattedTextToColumns = True

.WebConsecutiveDelimitersAsOne = True

.WebSingleBlockTextImport = False

.WebDisableDateRecognition = False

.WebDisableRedirections = False

.Refresh BackgroundQuery:=False

  End With

End Sub
```

The important portion of code is the below one, where we add a query table specifying the URL and the destination of the extracted data.

With ActiveSheet.QueryTables.Add(Connection:=_

"URL;http://sg.finance.yahoo.com/q/hp?s=FB", Destination:=Range("$A$1"))

With this, we can actually modify the vba code to make macro extract any stock we want as long as we have the stock code. We can do so by modifying the URL. For e.g. we can change the URL to,

"URL;http://sg.finance.yahoo.com/q/hp?s=GOOG", Destination:=Range("$A$2"))

What we have done is we are extracting Google stocks now and outputting it starting from A2 instead. Go ahead, change the code and re-run the macro. See what happens.

Now to make this a generic macro to extract any stock, insert the following codes in bold below into 'FBStockPrices'.

Sub FBStockPrices()

'

' FBStockPrices Macro

'

Dim stockCode As String

stockCode = Cells(1, 2).Value

    With ActiveSheet.QueryTables.Add(Connection:= _

    "URL;http://sg.finance.yahoo.com/q/hp?s=" & stockCode, Destination:=Range("$A$2"))

In the worksheet, we will reserve the first row to contain the stock code that we want to extract (fig. 71).

	A	B	C	D	E	F	G
1	Stock Code	GOOG					
2	Date	Open	High	Low	Close	Volume	Adj Close*
3		29-May-12	595.81	599.13	588.32	594.34	2,605,700	594.34
4		25-May-12	601	601.73	588.28	591.53	3,581,900	591.53
5		24-May-12	609.16	611.92	598.87	603.66	1,891,300	603.66
6		23-May-12	601.65	609.6	597.12	609.46	3,200,000	609.46
7		22-May-12	613.44	613.81	596	600.8	3,051,900	600.8
8		21-May-12	600.51	615.69	600	614.11	3,075,400	614.11
9		18-May-12	625.1	632.42	596.7	600.4	5,973,500	600.4
10		17-May-12	633.83	637.85	621.23	623.05	3,353,800	623.05
11		16-May-12	617.96	630.1	615.94	628.93	4,835,100	628.93
12		15-May-12	605.35	615	603.75	611.11	2,102,100	611.11
13		14-May-12	600.78	608.5	600.58	604	1,824,400	604
14		11-May-12	610.35	614.55	604.77	605.23	2,099,400	605.23

fig. 71

Explanation of Code

We first declare a String variable 'stockCode' to hold the stock code we want to extract.

Dim stockCode As String

The stock code is stored in cell B1. Assign that value into 'stockCode'.

stockCode = Cells(1, 2).Value

Now change the URL to accept 'stockCode' variable by concatenating it with the url web query. Next change the destination range to A2.

With ActiveSheet.QueryTables.Add(Connection:= _

"URL;http://sg.finance.yahoo.com/q/hp?s=" & stockCode, Destination:=Range("$A$2"))

Now experiment running the macro again this time. With this, you can quickly extract stock prices into your worksheets as long as you know the stock code. Try integrating this with the 'workbook_Open' event handler. Can you imagine the possibilities with Excel VBA?!

Chapter 14: Real World Case - Simple Financial Modeling Using Excel VBA

You have learned many aspects of Excel VBA programming. Now, we will integrate all that we have learned and apply them to some basic financial modeling. We will apply them to stock valuation and bond valuation, which means, trying to model or calculate what the price of the stock/bond should be and then comparing with the market price to determine if the stock is over valued or under valued.

Don't know much about stocks or bonds? Don't worry. I will try to give a simple explanation for each of them as we go along. The important thing is not understanding about the details of stocks and bonds. This is just an example. But rather, understand how i use Excel VBA to compute these financial formulas and you can use the same set of skills to compute complex formulas in other scenarios e.g. medicine, engineering.

Let's start with a Stock valuation example.

Stock Valuation using Excel

Stocks are issued by companies to raise capital. The stock price would rise or fall according to the company profits or losses. Companies also distribute income earned to stock holders through dividends. For e.g. a company declares a dividend of 1 cent for every stock owned. If you owned 10,000 stocks, you get 10000 * 0.01 = $100 dollars of dividend. One method of calculating a stock price is by measuring the dividends receiving and then discounting them. We need to discount them to account for the expected return percentage in a year. This method is called the dividend discount model or DDM.

Given investors can hold a stock for over a year, it is useful to value a stock over the investor's expected holding period. The formula is shown below.

Value of common equity

- $= \dfrac{D_1}{(1+k)^1} + \dfrac{D_2}{(1+k)^2} + \ldots + \dfrac{D_n}{(1+k)^n} + \dfrac{\text{Price at the end of the year n}}{(1+k)^n}$

Note: D = dividend, k = discount rate

Example: Calculate the value of a stock with a multiple-year holding period

An investor plans to hold Newco's stock for 2 years. Newco expects to pay its shareholders common equity, $0.25 per share over the next two years. The investor anticipates Newco's stock will close the end of that time period at $40 per share. Given a rate of return of 10%, what is the value of Newco's common stock at the end of the two-year time period?

Answer:
Value of Newco's common stock

$$= \frac{\$0.25}{(1.10)^1} + \frac{\$0.25}{(1.10)^2} + \frac{\$40}{(1.10)^2} = \$33.49$$

Creating the Model

Having understood the example, we first proceed to create the model in Excel. We will later then use Excel VBA to create the model and see the differences that Excel VBA can make. Create the labels as shown below (fig. 79).

	A	B	C	D	E
1	Stock Value	$33.50			
2	Dividend Per Year	$0.25			
3	Required Rate of Return on stock	10.00%			
4	No. of Years	2			
5	Final Price of Stock	40			
6					
7			Yr	Dividend	PV of Dividend
8			1	$0.25	$0.23
9			2	$0.25	$0.21

B1 fx =SUM(E8:E9)+B5/POWER((1+B3),B4)

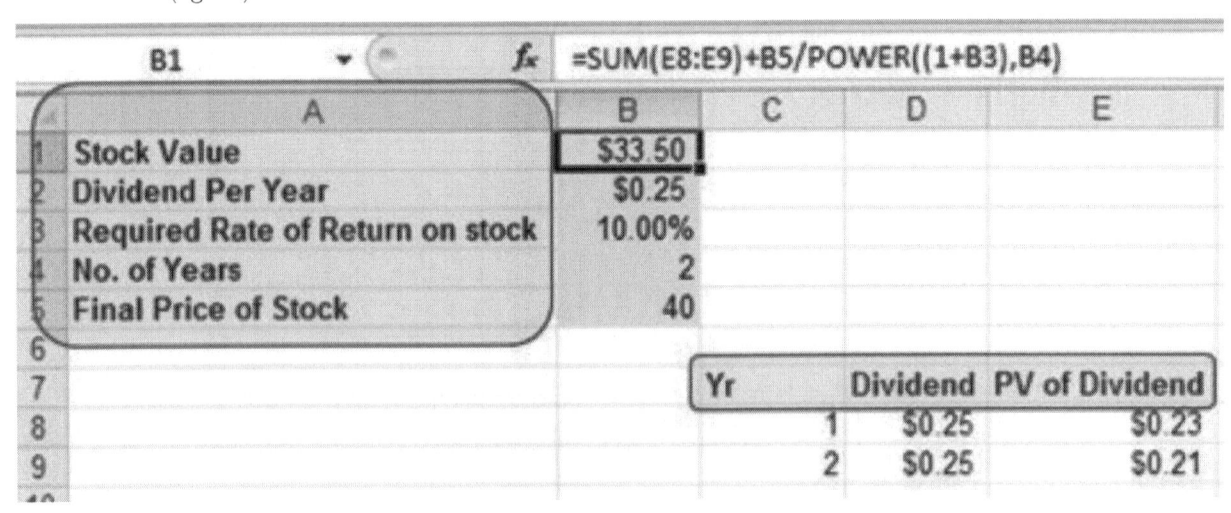

fig. 79

Highlight input/output cells with different colors (fig. 79b).

82

	B1		fx	=SUM(E8:E9)+B5/POWER((1+B3),B4)	
	A	B	C	D	E
1	Stock Value	$33.50			
2	Dividend Per Year	$0.25			
3	Required Rate of Return on stock	10.00%			
4	No. of Years	2			
5	Final Price of Stock	40			
6					
7			Yr	Dividend	PV of Dividend
8			1	$0.25	$0.23
9			2	$0.25	$0.21

fig. 79b

In the below highlighted excel sheet section, we aim to calculate the individual dividends present value (fig. 80). What is a present value? Imagine now you have a dollar. Is the worth of this dollar the same as if you receive a dollar in a year's time? No! You could have kept the dollar in a bank and earned some interest over the span of a year. Thus, a dollar that you will receive in the future is definitely valued less than a dollar. This is the present value of a dollar that you will receive in a year's time.

In figure 80, $0.25 in a year's time is valued as $0.23 now because we discount it by 10%, ($0.25/1.01). $0.25 received in two year's time is valued as $0.21 ($0.25/(1.01*1.01)). Unfortunately, we cannot go into present value too much as this is an Excel VBA course. To know more, get a Finance book!

	E8		fx	=D8/POWER((1+$B$3),C8)	
	A	B	C	D	E
1	Stock Value	$33.49			
2	Dividend Per Year	$0.25			
3	Required Rate of Return on stock	10.00%			
4	No. of Years	2			
5	Final Price of Stock	40			
6					
7			Yr	Dividend	PV of Dividend
8			1	$0.25	$0.23
9			2	$0.25	$0.21

fig. 80

Remember that the Stock Valuation formula is

$$= \frac{D_1}{(1+k)^1} + \frac{D_2}{(1+k)^2} + ... + \frac{D_n}{(1+k)^n} + \frac{\text{Price at the end of the year n}}{(1+k)^n}$$

Note the formula used to calculate the present value of the dividend and its references. =D8/POWER((1+$B$3),C8). Alternatively, you can use the PV (present value) function provided by Excel =PV($B$3,C8,0,-D8) (figure 81)

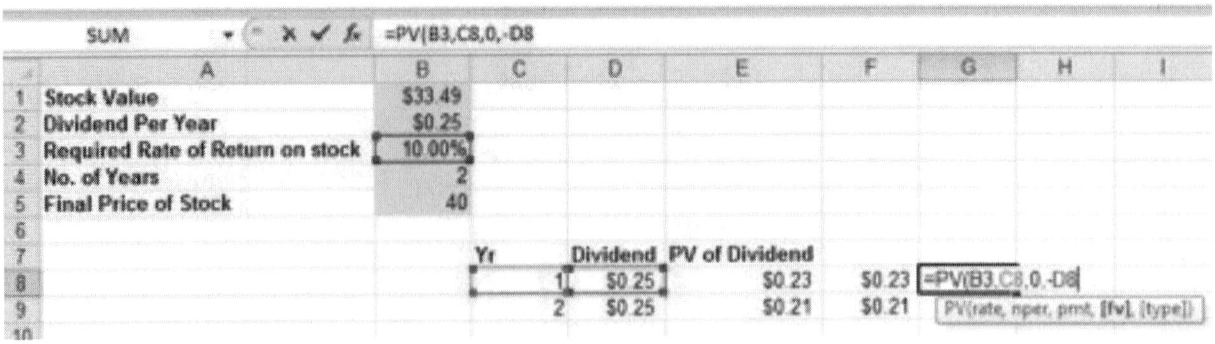

fig. 81

Sum the individual PVs of the dividends and of the final price of the stock to calculate our DDM value. Note that we have only two rows as the number of years is two.

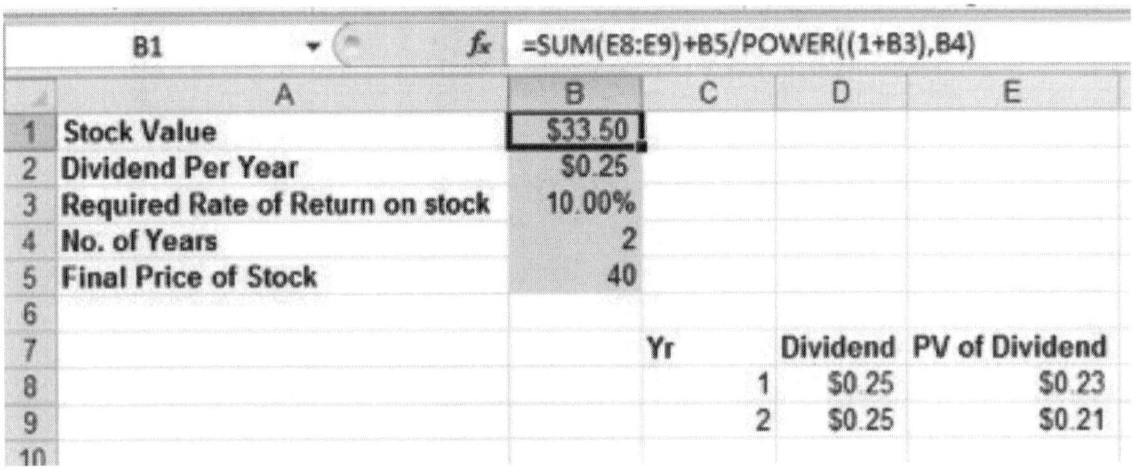

fig. 81b

The previous approach of calculating stock prices using DDM was quite manual and tedious. Imagine if we hold the stock for fifty years! We still have to manually enter dividends and calculate their present values.

Let's use Excel VBA to help us out!

Creating the Stock Valuation Model using Excel VBA

Create the below sub-routine in the DDM worksheet (fig. 82).

```
Sub calculateDDM()
    Dim dividend As Double
    Dim reqdReturn As Double
    Dim numOfYears As Integer
    Dim finalStockPrice As Double
    Dim sumOfPV As Double

    'take user input
    dividend = Cells(2, 2).Value
    reqdReturn = Cells(3, 2).Value
    numOfYears = Cells(4, 2).Value
    finalStockPrice = Cells(5, 2).Value

    'Generate dividend payouts and output them to Excel Sheet
    rowCounter = 8
    For counter = 1 To numOfYears
        Cells(rowCounter, 3).Value = counter
        Cells(rowCounter, 4).Value = dividend
        Cells(rowCounter, 5).Value = Application.WorksheetFunction.PV(reqdReturn, counter, 0, -dividend)
        sumOfPV = sumOfPV + Cells(rowCounter, 5).Value
        rowCounter = rowCounter + 1
    Next counter

    'Output final calculated Stock Price
    sumOfPV = sumOfPV + Application.WorksheetFunction.PV(reqdReturn, numOfYears, 0, -finalStockPrice)
    Cells(1, 2).Value = sumOfPV

    MsgBox "DDM Calculation Complete!"
End Sub
```

fig. 82

Run the Macro and notice that all your dividend entry rows as well as stock value is all calculated for you! Try changing the inputs and re-running the macro. The calculated prices will change accordingly. We have automated the Stock DDM calculation!

A	B	C	D	E
Stock Value	$12.38			
Dividend Per Year	$0.25			
Required Rate of Return on stock	10.00%			
No. of Years	6			
Final Price of Stock	20			
		Yr	Dividend	PV of Dividend
		1	0.25	0.227272727
		2	0.25	0.20661157
		3	0.25	0.1878287
		4	0.25	0.170753364
		5	0.25	0.155230331
		6	0.25	0.141118483

fig. 82b

Let's explain the code.

We create variables to store our user input and output values (fig. 82c).

```
Sub calculateDDM()
    Dim dividend As Double
    Dim reqdReturn As Double
    Dim numOfYears As Integer
    Dim finalStockPrice As Double
    Dim sumOfPV As Double

    'take user input
    dividend = Cells(2, 2).Value
    reqdReturn = Cells(3, 2).Value
    numOfYears = Cells(4, 2).Value
    finalStockPrice = Cells(5, 2).Value
```

fig. 82c

Assign user input values to the variables using 'Cells(row,column).Value'

```
Sub calculateDDM()
    Dim dividend As Double
    Dim reqdReturn As Double
    Dim numOfYears As Integer
    Dim finalStockPrice As Double
    Dim sumOfPV As Double

    'take user input
    dividend = Cells(2, 2).Value
    reqdReturn = Cells(3, 2).Value
    numOfYears = Cells(4, 2).Value
    finalStockPrice = Cells(5, 2).Value
```

fig. 83

We generate the dividend payout rows by looping from row 8 onwards to number of years.

```
'take user input
dividend = Cells(2, 2).Value
reqdReturn = Cells(3, 2).Value
numOfYears = Cells(4, 2).Value
finalStockPrice = Cells(5, 2).Value

'Generate dividend payouts and output them to Excel Sheet
rowCounter = 8
For counter = 1 To numOfYears
    Cells(rowCounter, 3).Value = counter
    Cells(rowCounter, 4).Value = dividend
    Cells(rowCounter, 5).Value = Application.WorksheetFunction.PV(reqdReturn, counter, 0, -dividend)
    sumOfPV = sumOfPV + Cells(rowCounter, 5).Value
    rowCounter = rowCounter + 1
Next counter
```

fig. 83b

In each iteration of the loop, we write to the excel sheet, the details of each year. We also calculate the present value of the dividend payout using the PV function from excel with 'Application.WorksheetFunction.PV'

fig. 84

'sumOfPV' variable accumulates the PVs of the dividend payouts

We then increment 'rowCounter' to point to the next row before starting a new iteration

```
'Generate dividend payouts and output them to Excel Sheet
rowCounter = 8
For counter = 1 To numOfYears
    Cells(rowCounter, 3).Value = counter
    Cells(rowCounter, 4).Value = dividend
    Cells(rowCounter, 5).Value = Application.WorksheetFunction.PV(reqdReturn, counter, 0, -dividend)
    sumOfPV = sumOfPV + Cells(rowCounter, 5).Value
    rowCounter = rowCounter + 1
Next counter
```

fig. 84b

Finally, sum up the sum of the PVs with the PV of the final stock price. That will be the calculated price of the stock.

Output it to Cell B1 and alert user with a message box.

```
'Output final calculated Stock Price
sumOfPV = sumOfPV + Application.WorksheetFunction.PV(reqdReturn, numOfYears, 0, -finalStockPrice)
Cells(1, 2).Value = sumOfPV

MsgBox "DDM Calculation Complete!"
```

fig. 84c

What We Have Learned

We have learned how to use Excel VBA to help us in complex calculations which involves calculating multiple rows and then taking the sum of them to determine the final output. This is an example which you can extend to other financial product calculations, such as loans, insurance, and of course other fields in engineering, medicine and the the sciences.

Going Further

Now that you have established basic fundamentals about Excel VBA programming, you can go on to apply them in your work and impress your boss!

I hope that this book benefits you and you will soon be on your way to getting your Excel VBA applications running in the world.

Feedback are always welcomed at support@i-ducate.com!

Printed in Great Britain
by Amazon.co.uk, Ltd.,
Marston Gate.